+ module each phase
Teach this book the first sem
Each student go through the ___
a one hour ___ tiny made
Desired outcomes. from the ___

Delivering Effective Training

Articles:
- Adult Learners (Analyze)
- Tray assessment (Analyze)
- ROI (Evaluation)

To Do -
*12/10 - Call Lech - make sure haven't ordered this book
in the computer. I haven't chosen my books yet
if any.*
92 Tray mtg - Establishing

Delivering Effective Training

Tom W. Goad

University Associates
8517 Production Avenue
San Diego, California 92121

Table of Contents

Table of Contents (continued)

Part V: Review

Introduction

One thought went into this book: to help *you* to become a better trainer. Regardless of whether you are to serve part time in a volunteer organization or full time in a large training department, regardless of the content that you want to teach, you are challenged to serve as a key instrument in the learning process. Learning lasts a lifetime. With increased technology and rapid change, learning is imperative just to "keep up" with our society. Thus, training has become an important and fast-growing field.

Being a good trainer, or facilitator, is not an easy task, but it does not require a formal degree in education or psychology. Experience helps, of course, but there are many new trainers who are very effective. What you do need is a desire to *help* other people to learn, patience, sufficient knowledge of your subject matter, and an understanding of the "tools of the trade." With these you can achieve highly effective and rewarding results. This book will acquaint you with the tools of the trade.

THE PURPOSE OF THIS BOOK

It is obvious that one book could not contain everything that everyone ever wanted to know about being a trainer. The book is, however, a condensation of key points taken from everyday training practice. It covers the spectrum: analyzing, designing, developing, conducting, and evaluating the components of training. Little of the material that is written about training is completely original, because although innovation in the training process is good—even sorely needed—the road to new things starts with the basics.

1

That is what this book is all about—the basics, with enough background to explain them. The next step is for you to use them.

This book is intended for anyone who is to perform the act of training. Although much of the technology included is based on training conducted within formal organizations such as corporations, government agencies, public agencies, and military establishments, the application generally is universal.

The ideal circumstance for the newly appointed trainer is to attend a formal "train the trainer" course, followed by an apprenticeship of observing and assisting. Because the ideal often remains just that, the material in this book, if used correctly, should serve as a reasonable substitute. Throughout the book are references that you can use to expand your knowledge and abilities as a trainer.

Old hands at the training game also will find utility in this book. It can serve as a refresher course and as a reference tool, pointing to more detail on subjects of interest. All skills need to be updated every now and then.

This book also can serve as a textbook for a formal trainer-training course. The chapters easily can be adapted for a course of a few hours duration as well as for one that takes several days.

ORGANIZATION OF THE BOOK

The chapters in the book are grouped into the general training subjects of background information, planning and preparation, presentation (implementation), and evaluation.

Introduction. The introductory chapters provide you with a framework for being a trainer; all contain important background information. These three chapters provide a definition and description of the training function (Chapter 1); a description of the roles filled by trainers (Chapter 2); and a nontechnical explanation of learning principles (Chapter 3).

Preparation. These chapters are designed to help you prepare for a training event. The three chapters provide information on the need to start the training properly (Chapter 4); how to prepare learning objectives and lesson plans (Chapter 5); and the preparation for and use of audiovisual aids (Chapter 6).

Implementation. These chapters are designed to help the trainer with various aspects of conducting training. They deal with the general theme of human relations, in recognition of the fact that interactions between people are at the heart of training. These six chapters include three on interpersonal communication: one on the basic subject of communication (Chapter 7); one on active listening as a communication tool (Chapter 8); and one on transactional analysis as a tool for dealing with individuals (Chapter 9). Chapter 10 discusses how to motivate learners; Chapter 11 presents ways to get learners involved in the training process; and Chapter 12 tells you how to deal with group dynamics.

Evaluation. A necessary and continuing element of the training process is evaluation. How to do it is the subject of Chapter 13.

Chapter 14 summarizes the key points of the book.

One of the attributes that makes, if not a great trainer, at least a good one, is organization. Just like a good story, training events should have a beginning, a middle, and an end. You should know where you are going and, more important, when you get there. This will be possible if you are well organized.

The chapters in this book are organized in a specific way to be most useful. Following the title and a brief description of each chapter, you will find several objectives. These are the criteria for your performance (reading) of the chapter. When you finish the chapter, you should know or be able to do these things. They serve as a road map, not only to help you to stay on track, but also to let you know when you have reached your destination. Some chapters contain materials that can be duplicated for your use in the future.

You are challenged to become further involved in the learning process by completing the exercises in each chapter. One of the cardinal rules of learning is that the learner *must* become involved. The learner is the person on the receiving end of instruction. You are the learner in this case and must, therefore, practice what you will be preaching. Completing the exercises is another way for you to become involved.

Many readers will not be satisfied to stop with these fourteen chapters. At some point, you will want to learn more about advanced training techniques. To accommodate you, a list of references is included with each chapter. These selected listings are by no means the only recommended sources, but they will provide you with a comprehensive training library.

HOW TO PROCEED

The best rule to follow is to proceed in whatever method suits you best. One approach is to read a chapter straight through, then to go back and take it more slowly. After the second time, try to answer any questions and complete any exercises without referring back to the text; then check your answers. Doing this will give you three shots at the material. Your chances of retaining something after three exposures are far better than after one or two. Try to apply the exercises to your actual training situation or do a little pretending—it still can do a lot of good. You also can use your own past experience on the receiving end of training as a resource.

ONE LAST WORD

Before you begin, here is a reminder. A good trainer (one who succeeds in helping a learner to learn) continually reviews everything that goes on in the training process. It is the only way to make sure that you have not forgotten anything or added an undesirable trait to your performance. Never assume that you have any methods and techniques so well rehearsed that they occur automatically every time you step into your trainer role. Periodically refresh yourself and your use of training tools. Your learners will be glad that you did.

PART I
INTRODUCTION TO TRAINING

Chapter 1
What Is Training?

Training, a human-resource development activity, is a closed-loop process. It includes numerous functions and can be accomplished in a variety of ways.

When you have completed this chapter, you will be able to:

- identify the five phases of the training cycle,
- describe several key activities of each phase,
- identify the most widely used methods of conducting training,
- differentiate between the trainer's and the learner's responsibilities for training.

INTRODUCTION TO TRAINING

People have been teaching and learning how to do things for quite a long time. Although our cave-dwelling predecessors are believed to have learned about fire by accident, subsequent generations most likely learned how to nurture it and cook with it through some form of training. Yet, interestingly enough, the field of training (also called adult education, human relations training, training and development, and human resource development) as a formal entity, a profession, is relatively new. Twentieth-century industrialization has accelerated the expansion and formalization of the training field, particularly in the areas of business and industry. The fact that our society continually is undergoing rapid change also has contributed to growing awareness of the need for training at many levels. Training comes in more flavors and styles than ice cream or automobiles. It is been used to solve many problems, it can help to make organizations run more smoothly, and, on occasion, it can be misused and create yet more problems. Toddlers receive training in the most basic areas of life. As people grow up, they are trained in how to drive, how to do their banking, and how to collect retirement benefits. Training is a necessary pastime in our highly technical, fast-moving, information-filled society.

The type of training that we think of most commonly is related to obtaining skills—how to do things. Technical, vocational, and other skill training occupies a large portion of the training spectrum. Personal improvement is a rapidly growing area of training. In addition, assertiveness training, stress-management training, and training in creative problem solving, as well as management training, now are used widely in organizations.

Training is provided to us through the organizations in which we work and through educational institutions (both public and private), professional associations, home study, television, and other media. The growing field of training serves human beings and their organizations in a myriad of ways. It contributes both directly and indirectly to the wellness and success of individuals and organizations.

The result is that we know much about training—what it is, how to do it—and are striving constantly to make it better. It is possible to be a perfectly capable trainer without ever being aware of many of the techniques and professional issues that are constantly arising within the expanding field. However, the broader your background in the total training function is, the better will be your understanding of the system in which you will be working. Gaining more knowledge of the many aspects of training will help you to determine where you fit. It also will help you to grow within this increasingly important field.

THE TRAINING CYCLE

Training can be treated as a total system, which is precisely how our military services—the biggest users of training—view it. The system can be thought of as a cycle with interrelated phases. These phases closely parallel the steps that a person would use in solving a problem. The phases are logical, following common sense. Although the particular phases of training identified by several different sources contain slight differences, in the end, they are all very similar.

In this discussion, we will examine five major phases:

1. *Analyze* to determine training requirements.
2. *Design* the training approach.
3. *Develop* the training materials.
4. *Conduct* the training.
5. *Evaluate* and update the training.

Phase 5 feeds back into Phase 1, making it a closed-loop system (see Figure 1). The evaluation phase can and should feed back into the four other phases as well. Training continually must be updated in order to be effective.

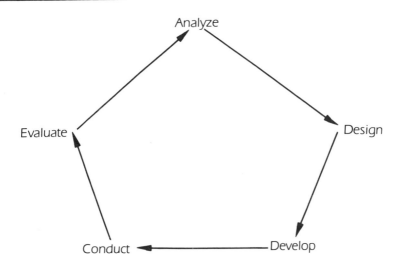

Figure 1. The Training Cycle As a Closed-Loop, Continuous System

A trainer does not perform every step of all five phases every time there is a training problem to be solved. The following discussion describes the kinds of tasks that a professional trainer might be asked to do.

Analyze To Determine Training Requirements

This phase is one of the two most overlooked in training (evaluation is the other). It has two primary purposes: (a) to determine that the training is needed in the first place and (b) to make sure that the training that does occur is based on sound, clearly identified requirements. Some of the steps of this phase are:

- identifying the problem and then determining if training is the best way to solve it (needs assessment is a popular term for this),
- analyzing the tasks and skills needed for the job or function for which the training is to be conducted,
- identifying the learners to be trained.

Design the Training Approach

The strategy for accomplishing the training is planned in the design phase. Like the analysis phase, it requires a great deal of data gathering. The more thorough the front-end analysis, the more complete and comprehensive the training design. Identifying good, sound objectives can make the difference between good training and wasting a lot of time in the name of training. Included in this phase are such tasks as:

- defining the learning objectives on which the training is to be based,
- determining the best (most appropriate) methods of training,
- selecting the best media for the training,
- identifying test items,
- determining prerequisites for the learners who are to receive the training,

- organizing the training—whether it be a half-day workshop or a multiple-week course—into its initial sequence, based on a variety of data.

Develop the Training Materials

The challenge here is to take the course outline that resulted from the design phase and to convert it into a complete set of materials that, when implemented, will result in the attainment of the desired learning objectives. This is where most of the time devoted to training (other than conducting the training) traditionally is spent. Depending on the circumstances, a wide variety of training materials may be needed. They might include:

- lesson plans (discussed in detail in Chapter 5)—used by the instructor, these also serve as specifications for developing other materials;
- learner materials—workbooks, lesson texts, programmed instruction texts, and handouts;
- audiovisual aids (the subject of Chapter 6)—films, slides, flip charts, transparencies, and so on;
- tests (discussed in Chapter 13)—based on items identified in the design phase;
- evaluation sheets.

Developing materials is not the only activity of this phase. Other activities include:

- making arrangements for the course and taking care of all the logistics and administrative details that can be done in advance,
- selecting and preparing the instructors/facilitators,
- molding the training events into practical blocks of instruction (this process may require several passes to make it complete),
- screening existing materials to discover what is usable,
- validating the training course and the materials as much as possible prior to the actual event.

Conduct the Training

This is where all the work becomes worth the effort. The trainer's role here will be to instruct, cajole, incite, coordinate, and otherwise facilitate the occurrence of learning. In addition to serving as training instructor and course/workshop coordinator, the trainer most likely will need to: (a) take care of logistics (see Chapter 4); (b) keep records of learner progress; (c) evaluate the training as it occurs; (d) evaluate the instructor performance; and (e) make on-line adjustments where needed.

Evaluate and Update the Training

This is the other often-neglected phase of training. Good training, to continue to be good, must be validated, updated, and then updated some more. This phase ends when the training course in question is no longer needed. Materials that have been used for any length of time without being reviewed are likely to be stale if not outdated. Every time a training event occurs is the time to improve it.

The activities of this phase include:

- instructor evaluation of the training after various segments are completed;
- learner evaluation of the course;
- third-party evaluation of the course;
- field evaluation, to determine if the learners are performing well in the roles for which the training was to have prepared them.

This phase feeds back into the other phases, making training a closed-loop system.

LEARNING OBJECTIVES

Learning for the sake of learning may be a nice indulgence, but it is a luxury that most people probably cannot afford. Training should have clearly stated objectives to guide it as well as the trainer. A widely used term for this is criterion-referenced instruction. Instructional systems development, the standard for military and other training, is based on performance objectives. Once the performance objectives are established, the training is conducted, then the effectiveness of the training is determined by checking to see whether or not the learners can achieve the objectives. Fully developed learning objectives have three parts: (a) a performance statement, (b) the conditions under which the performance is to be conducted, and (c) a standard—how well the performance is done. In other words, an objective tells the learner exactly what performance is expected—how well it should be performed, and under what conditions (for example, to be able to recite the rules for safe operation of an electronic widget, without any cues and with no mistakes).

The training effort should be geared to achieve the objectives, no more or less than this. The development and use of performance objectives are discussed in detail in Chapter 5.

TYPES OF TRAINING

Training is of two general types: that controlled by the instructor and that controlled by the learner. An example of the former is the lecture—the most widely used form of instruction. A home study course featuring programmed learning texts is a good example of the latter. For all practical purposes, however, all learning ultimately is controlled by the learner.

The following is an overview of several types of training.

Classroom

This can take many forms, ranging from the lecture situation in which the trainer stands and does all the talking to a situation in which the trainer merely steps in occasionally to keep things going. There are indications that the second method produces more effective learning, and this will be discussed later in this book.

Programmed Learning

This is also called programmed instruction. It most often features a programmed instructional text, in which the learner is guided through the material and required to satisfactorily answer questions and work problems before moving on. Various machines and audiovisual devices also are used for this type of training.

Computer-Assisted Instruction

Often called CAI, this is the automated version of programmed learning. Home computers have helped to revive this form of training, in which the learner sits at a computer terminal and interacts with the computer to complete the training lessons. Computer and audiovisual technology have made possible some highly sophisticated variations of training in this area.

Laboratory

In the laboratory method, learners participate by taking actions similar to or identical with those that they will be taking on completion of the training. Examples of this are law students holding mock court, operators manipulating pieces of equipment, and salespersons practicing their newly learned techniques on one another.

Structured Experiences

Often referred to as learning games, these activities are carefully planned to produce a particular type of learning. Examples are communication experiments, team competitions that involve negotiation, and other activities in which the participants learn something by doing and experiencing. The activity need not be based on reality, as long as the experience can produce real learning.

Simulation

This technique is used to supplement, enhance, and sometimes replace live training in a particular situation or for a particular device or machine. The variety of simulation activities ranges from the quasi-real, such as an "in-basket" activity that is used to train managers in decision making, to the very realistic flight simulation that is used to train pilots, not only in the basics but also in how to deal with emergency conditions in the aircraft.

Case Studies

This is similar to games and simulations. Learners develop solutions and approaches to situations that are presented by means of written cases. Proposed and actual solutions and their results then are discussed. The case-study method is quite popular in management and business training.

Role Playing

Learners are asked to act out certain roles (e.g., a disgruntled customer) in order for other learners to be able to practice how to handle such problem cases. In this way, participants can be exposed to both sides of an issue. This is one of the training methods that offers learners the opportunity to be more involved in the learning process.

INSTRUCTIONAL MEDIA

A variety of instructional media can be used to spice up the learning environment. In addition, audiovisual and other training aids can be of great assistance in presenting material in the most interesting and informative manner.

Some of the types of training mentioned previously, such as simulators and computer-assisted instruction, actually are forms of training media. Other forms of media usually are classified in the area of audiovisuals—film, videotape, slides, filmstrips, cassette tapes. Other training aids include overhead projectors, newsprint flip charts on easels, mockups of actual devices, and the old standby: the chalkboard. Experience has taught us that an appropriate multimedia approach can be very successful. You will learn more about audiovisual aids in Chapter 6.

RESPONSIBILITY FOR LEARNING

Simply stated, if the learner is a changed person as a result of the instructional process—"changed" meaning being capable of achieving the objectives of the training—then the training, no matter what transpired, is successful. With experience, your intuition will enable you to determine if learning has taken place. If you use the tools described in this book and adopt a total systems approach to training, you will facilitate the training in which you are involved from a solid, secure base.

It already has been said, and not for the last time, that the learner has the ultimate responsibility for whether or not learning takes place. If you do your best to facilitate the process, the odds are that you will be able to help the learner to learn something worthwhile.

SUMMARY

Training is a total system function. It is a process or cycle. It has a variety of applications and comes in a variety of types. The key points in regard to training are:

1. Training is a closed-loop process consisting of five phases: analyze, design, develop, conduct, and evaluate.
2. Each of these important phases consists of numerous steps, part or all of which may be required for a given training event.
3. Training can be applied in a variety of ways.
4. There are many types of training, and the ones to be used for a particular situation depend on a variety of factors.
5. The ultimate responsibility for learning rests with the learner; the responsibility of the trainer is to do whatever is possible to enable the learning process to happen most easily and effectively.

SELECTED REFERENCES

Many books and journals have been published in the field of training and development and in related areas. A number of excellent publishing organizations specialize in just these kinds of materials. Several professional associations also offer materials and other assistance. Of particular interest is the American Society for Training and Development (ASTD), Suite 305, 600 Maryland Avenue, S.W., Washington, DC 20024. ASTD has local chapters that hold regular meetings and professional growth events. It also publishes the *Training and Development Journal.* This, along with *Training* magazine (Lakewood Publications, 731 Hennepin Avenue, Minneapolis, Minnesota 55403) are two widely distributed publications that offer guidance to and communication among trainers.

The following books offer a good overview of the training profession:

Davis, L.N. *Planning, conducting, and evaluating workshops.* San Diego, CA: Learning Concepts, 1974.

Craig, R.L. (Ed.). *Training and development handbook* (2nd ed.). New York: McGraw-Hill, 1976.

Mager, R.F., & Beach, K.M., Jr. *Developing vocational instruction.* Belmont, CA: Fearon-Pitman, 1967.

Chapter 2
The Roles of the Trainer

Training is far more than standing in front of a group of learners and conveying information. A person of many roles, the trainer is most of all a facilitator.

When you have completed this chapter, you will be able to:

- identify the major roles that a trainer may be called on to fill,
- explain the significance of functioning as a *facilitator* of learning (the trainer's primary role).

FLEXIBILITY IS IMPORTANT

There are times when the obvious parts of training, such as instructing, may be the least important. In a training workshop in which the learners are having a hot and heavy discussion about a key point in the training, a good trainer will not jump in and say, "Enough, it's time for me to train some more." By being more than a conveyor of knowledge, a good trainer probably caused the give and take in the first place and would recognize when such a discussion was, in itself, a source of learning. When working with a learner who is having difficulty in understanding the point of the training, the trainer will have to use a different style. This is one of the reasons why trainers often are referred to as "facilitators." The purpose of any training is to facilitate learning, and it may well require a switching of roles and styles in order to accomplish that in any given situation.

From the types of tasks listed under the descriptions of the five training phases (in Chapter 1), you can see that a

21

trainer must have a repertoire of diverse roles. As you gain experience in training, you will begin to see indications that it is time to switch from one role to another. Your actions and reactions will become more spontaneous, and flexibility will become more a natural part of your performance. The skills required to fill the diverse roles that you will be required to play and the sense of timing that you will need to use them appropriately will begin to seem less like individual things to turn on and off at will and more like a naturally flowing process.

Everyone has to face the fact that he or she may not be very good at some of the roles that people are called on to perform. One person may always goof up the movie projector. Another may never feel comfortable or effective in counseling a troubled learner. This does not mean that these people should give up their chosen profession. The secret is to concentrate on your strong suit. When in doubt, stick with the things that you know and do best. If you are successful in one area, you will be more likely to try new things and to attempt to be innovative as you progress and polish your skills.

FACILITATION IS A COMPOSITE ROLE

Facilitating involves utilizing all your abilities and available resources in order to provide the best access to the knowledge and skills that the training is designed to impart.

When you become competent in filling any one of several different roles, depending on the situation, you will decide what will bring the best results and will exploit that characteristic. You will become familiar with the tools available to you and will know when to use them. If you recognize from the beginning that the learner, too, is an important member of the learning team, you will begin to see training as a synergistic system in which the whole is greater than the sum of the parts. Facilitation, then, is an attitude as well as a job.

There is no one best way to facilitate learning. In some cases, it simply is a matter of reserving a meeting room and renting a projector. If you need to recruit instructors, the job may become a little more complicated. If the workshop is not going well, and the learners are grumbling, facilitating becomes a downright challenge.

As a trainer, you may have to decide whether to function as a manager or as an operator. The trainer as manager lets the learner do all the work, merely oversees the project, and intervenes on occasion to give the learner direction. In view of the popularity and success of self-paced, or individualized, instruction, this can be very effective. Of course, the trainer as manager also is involved in the other four phases of training (analysis, design, development, and evaluation). This could involve overseeing an internal staff or dealing with outside consultants. The instructor as operator, in contrast, ends up with the proverbial dirty hands, taking much of the responsibility of learning for the learner. This means doing a lot of demonstration and telling—leading the learner through the process.

As you may have guessed by now, a true facilitator of learning, is both a manager and an operator. A person who is learning to be an airplane pilot receives a great deal of lecture and demonstration in theory and techniques before being allowed to enter a cockpit, and the reason for this is obvious to all. The point is, there is an appropriate time and place for each type of instruction. Learning to recognize when each style is appropriate and learning to be able to blend them most effectively is one of the most important achievements of a training facilitator.

There are many other roles that the trainer may be called on to fill. Among them are:

subject-matter expert	follower
counselor	friend
leader/motivator	detail person
learner	handy-person
psychologist	synthesizer
manager	performer
human being	planner
listener	realist
role model	evaluator

investigator	catalyst
creator	thinker
"go fer"	autocrat
producer	benevolent dictator
decision maker	researcher

Once again, the more roles that you can fill as needed, the more successful you will be as a facilitator of learning. A few key roles that you undoubtedly will need to fill are: subject-matter expert, counselor, leader/motivator, learner, psychologist, manager, and human being.

Subject-Matter Expert

The more technical or specific the topic of training is, the more important it is that someone be able to answer detailed, technical questions. It helps if that person is the trainer. It is a good idea to learn all you can about the subject of the training, especially if it is directly related to your organization's product or service. If the subject is highly technical or highly specialized, you probably will have to rely on others to serve as "experts." It is important to remember that the learners will assume that you know just about all there is to know on the subject. They will accept it when you admit that you do not know the answers to some questions, especially if you promise to obtain the information. However, if you are challenged frequently in a training situation, and you cannot set the issues at rest, it may well affect the efficacy of the training.

Counselor

EX. - Time Card Tory Procurement Integrity FOE

Whenever you deal with human beings, you deal with situations in which someone may need help from time to time. You can ignore the personal problems of individuals in a training group on the grounds that you are being paid to be a trainer, not a counselor. The fact remains that some learners will have problems that make it difficult for them to achieve their learning objectives. If you can counsel these people and help to create a climate in which they can

During breaks - will ask questions - request guidance "what would you do" - A good counselor facilitates learning - share the principles - let them discover.

achieve success, then it is "training" time well spent. You may be called on merely to *listen* for a few minutes. The learner may have a problem that can be helped simply by talking about it or the learner may be approaching the learning situation in the wrong way. If you can help in cases like these, by all means, you should do so. (You probably will want to improve the skills described in Chapter 8, Active Listening.)

Leader/Motivator

It is difficult for a trainer to pull back within the training setting without actually pulling a disappearing act. You are the leader—at least during the time that the training is conducted. All learners need some guidance, and even learning materials that are designed to be self-paced may need some explanation. Learners generally will insist on having someone to whom they can look for direction.

The type of leadership you exert will depend on your preferences, the nature of the learning situation, and the learners within it. A more democratic approach generally achieves more positive results and leaves the learners with more agreeable feelings about the experience. If there is a shortage of time, however, you may need to be more autocratic in order to complete the training. (Chapter 10 contains information on using the leadership role to motivate learners.)

[handwritten marginalia: and your leadership style. Maybe provide instrument]

Learner

[handwritten note: Situational leadership - Important to know your primary leadership style]

Because of rapidly advancing technology, constant change, and the information explosion, and because of the nature of many people, learning is a lifelong avocation for most of us. An exciting part of being a trainer is that there is much to be learned from the learners, not the least of which is in the area of human nature and behavior. You almost always can learn something interesting—and useful—that you did not know from someone whom you are supposed to be training. In addition, the group's process or the group's discussion

[handwritten note: you benefit and it also gives you a chance to reaffirm people's learning, experience and self-esteem]

sometimes will go in a direction that you had not anticipated, and there can be a great deal of learning in these unexpected developments. The learners will have a lot more respect for you when they realize that you, too, can be open to learning.

Psychologist

Psychology is not just for "shrinks." We have but to use any of our senses in the presence of another human being and we are using psychology. It is not necessary to become a specialist in educational psychology or learning theory in order to be an effective trainer, but knowing that feedback is vital to learning certainly would not hurt any trainer's performance. The information in Chapter 3, Learning Theory, and Chapter 12, Group Dynamics, is an example of the ways in which trainers can apply selected aspects of the field of psychology to the benefit of themselves and their learners.

Manager

Managing is not merely the act of getting things done through others, of being the boss. Functions, tasks, and projects must be administered; funds must be accounted for; and resources must be used in the most efficient and effective manner. Even a new trainer has things to manage (time, whatever resources are to be used) and must make certain that his or her task, no matter how trivial, fits into the overall scheme of things. Every step of the training process mentioned in Chapter 1 must be managed; someone must accept responsibility for seeing that the task is completed on time, within the budget, and according to plan. As tasks grow in size and complexity, the role of trainer as manager becomes more of a challenge.

Human Being

We all are familiar with the teacher who constantly reminds the students that they know so much less than the teacher, or the one who acts as though he or she were doing the learners a favor in letting them partake of the knowledge that the teacher is sharing. A teacher, or trainer, is no more or less human than each person in the learning group. Trainers err, on occasion. Because the learners are human, too, they generally will understand and forgive (as well as survive) your mistakes.

. . . And More

The following is a list of miscellaneous activities performed by trainers at one time or another. They are included to help paint the picture of what a trainer does. More information on what each activity is and how to perform it is found in the chapter(s) indicated.

Activity	Chapter(s)
Prepare	3, 4, 5, 6
Use audiovisual/training aids	6
Communicate	7, 8, 9
Get learners involved/motivate	10, 11
Control the group/handle problems	12
Test, evaluate	13

EXERCISE

Review a typical, past experience in a training situation in which you were one of the *learners*. Think of the trainer who was involved in terms of the list of roles shown on pages 23 and 24 and concentrate on the seven key roles (subject-matter expert, counselor, leader/motivator, learner, psychologist, manager, and human being).

1. List each role that the trainer filled at one time or another in your experience.

2. For each role listed, answer the following questions:
   a. Did it make a positive contribution to learning?
   b. Why did it or did it not?

3. For those roles that were not filled (especially from the list of the seven key ones), determine whether or not there were circumstances in which it would have helped if the trainer had filled one or more of the roles. How would it have helped?

SUMMARY

The trainer is a person of many roles, the most important one being that of facilitator of the learning process. This is the function of doing everything possible—and that varies—to cause learning to take place. The secret is to develop skill in using a wide variety of training tools and in expanding the roles that one fills. Some of the most critical roles of the trainer are:

- subject-matter expert—who works closely with other experts, especially in training-event preparation;
- counselor—who helps learners through the learning process;
- leader/motivator—of learners and of other trainers;
- psychologist—who deals with many different people;
- manager—of yourself and your functions as well as of other persons;
- human being—who is just like the learners.

SELECTED REFERENCES

The following sources contain material on the role of the trainer. The book by Davies also contains an excellent bibliography.

Craig, R.L. (Ed.). *Training and development handbook* (2nd ed.). New York: McGraw-Hill, 1976.

Davies, I.K. *Instructional technique.* New York: McGraw-Hill, 1981.

Knowles, M. *Self-directed learning.* Chicago: Association Press/ Follett, 1975.

Pfeiffer, J.W., & Jones, J.E. (Eds.). *The annual handbook for group facilitators* (10 vols.). San Diego, CA: University Associates, 1972-1981.

Pfeiffer, J.W., & Goodstein, L.D. *The annual for facilitators, trainers, and consultants.* San Diego, CA: University Associates, 1982.

Pinto, P.R., & Walker, J.W. *A study of training development roles and competencies.* Washington, DC: American Society for Training and Development, 1978.

Chapter 3
Learning Theory

The instructional process is part of a larger system, the learning process. Acquiring some knowledge about how people learn is one of the first steps of the wise trainer.

When you have completed this chapter, you will be able to:

- describe why a background in basic learning theory is important to the trainer,
- state the basic tenets of adult learning theory and why it is so important to the trainer,
- explain and apply some key principles of learning.

THEORY IS BASED ON OBSERVATION

Learning theory is based on sound, field-tested, and—in many cases—long-standing principles. You may be surprised to discover that you already are familiar with many of them. After all, we have been on the receiving end of many of these concepts for most of our lives.

Fortunately, there is a lot of research data available on how, why, and when people learn. Learning psychologists, educators, and human-resource-development specialists all have been conducting research for many years. The result is that we can state, with a good deal of confidence, principles that you can follow to achieve maximum learning in given situations. Many of these principles have been organized into various theories. These theories can be divided into two general categories: stimulus-response and cognitive. Most of us have heard of Pavlov, who conditioned his dog to salivate at the ringing of a bell—an extreme

31

example of the stimulus-response, or conditioning, theories. This also is called behavior modification. The idea is that if the subject receives the proper stimulus, the response will be the desired one. Cognitive theories deal more with the acquisition of knowledge and are more humanistic in nature. They generally rely on the individual to learn through self-motivation.

TYPES OF LEARNING

There are several ways to classify types of learning. Table 1 shows a classification that is used by the military establishment.

Table 1. Learning Categories and Subcategories

Learning Category	Learning Subcategory
I. Mental Skill	1. Learning and using rules 2. Classifying-recognizing patterns 3. Identifying symbols 4. Detecting 5. Making decisions
II. Information	6. Recalling bodies of knowledge
III. Physical skill	7. Performing gross motor skills 8. Steering and guiding-continuous movement 9. Positioning movement and recalling procedures 10. Voice communicating
IV. Attitude	11. Attitude learning

Taken from "Interservice Procedures for Instructional Systems Development" (AD-A019486-19490). Available from National Technical Information Service, 5285 Port Royal Road, Springfield, VA 22161. This series of documents, adopted by all the services, provides detailed guidelines for the total process of developing and implementing military training programs and systems. Most of the guidelines, including these learning categories, are applicable to just about any type of training.

There is an even simpler way to categorize learning into three groups:

- cognitive
- psychomotor, and
- affective.

Cognitive

This means *knowledge* learning. These are the mental skills and information shown in Table 1. When you learned your multiplication tables and how to parse a sentence in elementary school, you were acquiring cognitive skills. If you are serving as a trainer in a lecture situation, you will be facilitating the acquisition of cognitive learning. Such learning also is acquired through individualized training such as programmed texts and computer-assisted instruction.

Psychomotor

These are the manipulative, or physical, skills that are required to *do* something. Whereas cognitive learning would be used to know the rules for safe operation of a moped, psychomotor skills are required to actually ride one. The most common uses of physical skills are shown in Table 1. Laboratory settings, in which the learners receive hands-on training, are best for gaining physical skills. These types of training include simluation, on-the-job training, and practice sessions in which learners actually manipulate a machine or device. Lecture and related cognitive training can only help to prepare a learner for learning physical skills. The ultimate learning requires a setting in which actual performance takes place.

Affective

These skills are related to attitudes, values, and interests. Developing attitude skills means causing changes in how much the learner appreciates the subject. Personal leadership or example, such as the trainer as subject-matter expert, is one recognized way to facilitate attitudinal learning. For example, this type of learning is used by the "big brother" organizations in their work with young people.

We know that attitudes are learned and we know the importance of attitudes in the work place and in everything we do. However, affective, or attitudinal, training is more difficult to do than other types of training—in part, because it is so difficult to measure.

EXERCISE

Following is a list of things that a learner might be required to do. Match each of them with one of the three types of learning: cognitive (knowledge), psychomotor (physical skill), or affective (attitude). Then break them down further according to the learning subcategories shown in Table 1.

Category	Subcategory	
		1. Stating the reasons why a supervisor should avoid berating a subordinate in front of others.
		2. Communicating with the radio tower the appropriate check-in message.
		3. Moving blocks from one basket to another.
		4. Exemplifying the pride of the Marine Corps while on shore leave.
		5. Riding a unicycle.
		6. Determining whether a situation is a routine labor dispute or one that involves affirmative action.
		7. Motivating employees to arrive at work on time.

Category	Subcategory	
		8. Identifying subordinates who have potential drinking problems.
		9. Reciting the rules for safe operation of a drill press.
		10. Following correct, safe procedures in conducting preflight operations on a 747.

The answers to this exercise can be found at the end of this chapter.

ASPECTS OF LEARNING

An additional contribution of the monumental amount of psychological research is that we know that there are a number of aspects of learning related to human behavior and how the brain works. One of these aspects is memory. Memory plays an important role in learning. Some pieces of input go into short-term memory; others go into long-term memory. When a person performs a memory learning task such as recalling a set of rules, retrieval of that information must be successful if the memory is to be reinforced, i.e., learned. This is closely related to the concept of extinction. Information eventually will disappear from a person's memory if it is not used.

Memory can be greatly enhanced (that is, it can be moved from short-term to long-term storage) through review and practice. There are a variety of tricks that can help people to commit things to memory; the process itself is called mnemonics. Divising schemes of abbreviations or associations for remembering lists or rules is one example of such techniques.

Another concept is that learning proceeds in a predictable manner. People do not learn at a constant, steady rate. There are, instead, peaks and valleys in individual progress. This means that it may be quite all right if learners have difficulty at times because breakthroughs soon will be achieved.

Most learners desire orderliness. It, too, enhances the learning process. Dividing learning tasks into chunks is also conducive to better learning. It entails an orderly buildup of a reasonable amount of material at a time, reinforced through review, recitation, and practice, until the whole is mastered.

Another means of learning is observation. On-the-job training, for instance, generally is the process of observing an experienced person doing something and then trying it oneself. All of our senses take in a vast amount of observed data that contribute to the learning process.

People learn better when practice is distributed than they do from cramming. Research has shown that regular, periodic study produces better results on a final examination than does a cramming session shortly before the test.

Research now being conducted offers the possibility of yet more knowledge regarding how people learn. One theory is that everything that enters a person's memory remains in there somewhere. The problem is to gain access to it.

Basic Principles

The following is a synthesis of proven and useful principles regarding learning, presented from the point of view of the person who is attempting to facilitate learning. The most widely recognized principles appear first. The best approach is to integrate principles from all the approaches. There is no such thing as one best theory of learning.

Informing the Learner of the Learning Objective

There should be no doubt in the learner's mind about what is expected to be learned and what should be the result of the training session. (See Chapter 5 for more on learning objectives.)

Practice

"Practice makes perfect," and practice should be distributed in an orderly manner. This applies to cognitive learning as well as to psychomotor skills learning.

Guidance and Prompting

This is the process of assisting the learner through the learning process, rather than relying on osmosis. Guidance can be offered simply by asking a question or it can be a formal preplanned exercise. It does *not* involve doing the work for the learner.

Feedback

Feedback in training is when you, the trainer, indicate to the learner the degree of progress that the learner is achieving. If you ask a question and the learner answers it correctly, the feedback occurs when you tell the learner (or indicate in some other manner) that the question was answered properly. The sooner this occurs, the better. Without feedback, you can assume that learning does not take place. A learner needs to know when things are not going well, although often it is not necessary to feed this back because the learner already is aware of the difficulty. On the other hand, giving positive feedback is one of the best things you can do for a learner. People like and need to be told when they are doing well. Use positive feedback with abandon. Feedback is one of the most important elements of communication. (This is discussed further in Chapter 7.)

Transfer of Learning

Think back to your own school experience. You transferred your learning of basic arithmetic to algebra and perhaps to other forms of math. You still transfer that learning whenever you balance your checkbook. This is a key point of learning:

that one aspect of learning builds on previous aspects. Future learning sessions will take advantage of sessions already completed. For example, having learned how to type, a person can transfer many of those skills to learning how to use word-processing equipment.

Activities Related to the Learning Objectives

That learning activities should be related to learning objectives seems obvious. You might be surprised, however, to see how many instructors include such things as movies or reading sessions as fillers when it would have been better to have dismissed the learners early or to have gone on to the next subject.

Making a Good First Impression

Trainers should not present themselves as infallible, but they should appear to be competent and prepared. A trainer who makes an obvious error during a first session can make a strong and lasting (negative) impression on the learners. This obviously can affect the rest of the training.

Enthusiasm

People learn most and best in a positive learning environment. Intimidation and sternness no longer are seen as facilitative to learning. Enthusiasm, when accompanied by exciting learning experiences and good feelings, can overcome many shortcomings, especially for an inexperienced trainer.

EXERCISE

Outline a brief training activity that you believe would help a learner to learn how to perform each of the following objectives. For example, a learning activity for the objective "State the safety rules for operating a body scanning device" might be to have the learner recite the rules and give a reason for each one. Many activities can be used to achieve most objectives, so do not feel that there must be one best answer. A *sample* activity for each objective is provided at the end of this chapter.

1. Stating the reasons why a supervisor should avoid berating a subordinate in front of others.

2. Communicating with the radio tower the appropriate airplane check-in message.

3. Moving blocks from one basket to another.

4. Exemplifying the pride of the Marine Corps while on shore leave.

5. Riding a unicycle.

6. Determining whether a situation is a routine labor dispute or one that involves affirmative action.

7. Motivating employees to arrive at work on time.

8. Identifying subordinates who have potential drinking problems.

9. Reciting the rules for safe operation of a drill press.

10. Following correct, safe procedures in conducting preflight operations on a 747.

ADULT LEARNING

Andragogy is the newly-emerging concept of adult education. According to Malcolm Knowles, an eminent theorist and practitioner in the field of adult education, the adult learner is a neglected species.[1] Past research in the areas of education and training has been focused on children and animals. Yet, learning is a process—as opposed to a series of finite, unrelated steps—that lasts throughout the entire life span of most human beings.

We do have data regarding how adults learn. At the heart of the concept of andragogy (as opposed to pedagogy, or youth learning), is the assumption that adults want to learn. It is safe to assume that they show up for training because they desire to learn something (provided, of course, that what you have to offer is what they came to get). If this is the case, then you have a contract. It is their responsibility, and they will gladly accept it. Even if they were told to come, it most likely was because of their professional roles, and they chose their professions themselves.

If you have any doubts about this, talk to friends who are taking university graduate courses for adults or courses in photography or the like at a local YMCA or community adult center. They will talk in terms of "no-nonsense" teaching/learning and make it clear that if they were not gaining benefit—learning—they would walk out of the session. You probably have had similar personal experience in adult-oriented learning situations.

The Peer Concept

As a professional trainer, you frequently will be dealing with people who are professionals in their own fields. A positive approach is to make it clear that you and the participants are equal. It just so happens that you have some knowledge and skills available that, when obtained by the learners, will merely add to their growing lists of

---

[1]Malcolm Knowles, *The Adult Learner: A Neglected Species* (2nd ed.). Houston, TX: Gulf, 1978.

accomplishments. In other words, avoid putting yourself on a pedestal. Let the learners know that you are aware of (and respect) the knowledge that they do have.

Adults Are Different

- Adults learn by doing; they want to be *involved*. Never merely demonstrate how to do something if an adult learner actually can perform the task, even if coaching is involved and it takes longer that way.
- Problems and examples must be realistic and relevant to the learners.
- Adults relate their learning to what they already know. This will be very pronounced with some people and can cause problems. If you can get in touch with the backgrounds of your particular learners and can give examples that they can relate to, they will love you for it—and they will learn more easily.
- An informal environment is best. Trying to intimidate adults causes tension, and tension inhibits learning.
- Variety stimulates and tends to open up all five of the learner's senses. Change the pace and the technique from time to time.
- Do not implement any type of grading system (unless the nature of your training absolutely requires it). Learning flourishes in a win-win, no-grades environment. Instead, offer plenty of guidance when and where it is needed. Checking learning objectives is for more effective than assigning a grade.
- A facilitator of the adult learning process is a change agent. Your role is to present information (or skills) in an environment that is conducive to learning. The learner's role is to take that information (or skills) and apply it in the way that is best for them. The responsibility for facilitating is yours. The responsibility for learning is theirs.

Traditional learning, especially in public education, is oriented toward the teacher imparting knowledge to the students. Adult learning is the process of one person (the trainer) providing the opportunity for another person (the adult learner) to acquire knowledge and skills. The traditional approach says "Here is what you need; now take it and remember it." The adult approach says "Here it is; you will take it if you believe that it will benefit you." Adults have more *choice* in the matter and they are more used to exercising choice. In fact, there are some people who think that the principles of adult learning described here might well be applied to younger learners.

EXERCISE

Think back to learning situations that you have been in that you enjoyed thoroughly and felt that you got a lot out of. List the reasons why you felt this way.

Now compare these items with the principles of adult learning as well as with the learning principles stated previously. Very likely there are some strong similarities. Then, for comparison, think of experiences you have had in which you were disappointed in what you learned or in how the training was conducted. Now critique these in light of the principles and concepts presented in this book.

THE THREE R'S OF TRAINING

Historically, traditional education has been noted for its three R's: reading, 'riting, and 'rithmetic. In a sense, training has its three R's, too. They are:

- repetition,
- reiteration,
- rote.

A lot of statistics have been compiled over the years to support these practices. When things are repeated (three times seems to be very effective), the learner's retention rate increases. Repeating something three times causes people to remember it longer. Things just stick with you longer when you have repeated them three times. Get the message?

Of course, a trainer would not want to just stand on a platform and say every key point three times. Part of training preparation (which is discussed more fully in the next chapter) consists of laying out ways to emphasize the key points of the training. Variety is important, both for you and for the learner. There are several ways to achieve this. You can state the item from more than one point of view, express it in an example, have the learner state the item back to you by asking pertinent questions, and so on. Visual aids and end-of-session summaries provide excellent means by which to place emphasis when you want it. You also can suggest that salient points be taken down as notes.

Concentration on the key points should help to simplify your learning session, and this holds true whether the session is a lecture or a laboratory. You will find, if the training-preparation process is complete, that the process of repetition, of emphasizing key points, becomes easy to do.

There is an old saying from military training that goes something like this: "Tell them what you're going to tell them, tell them, and then tell them what you've told them." Perhaps a better way to say this is: "Let the learners know what the learning objectives are; present the material needed for them to achieve the objectives; and then give them the opportunity to practice, and validate, their performance of the objectives. This is a tried-and-true process.

SUMMARY

Principles about how people learn are based largely on common sense. Some of the key points from this chapter are:

1. There are three types of learning: cognitive (knowledge), psychomotor (physical), and affective (attitudes and values).

2. Some basic learning principles are: state the learning objectives; use practice; give guidance and prompting; give feedback; take advantage of the transfer of learning ; relate activities to the learning objectives; make a good first impression; and show enthusiasm.

3. Adults learn because they choose to learn.

4. Repetition is an important part of the learning process.

SELECTED REFERENCES

Much material on learning theory and principles is academically oriented. Any basic, college psychology text, of which there are many, will provide a great deal of information on the learning process. Because so many of these textbooks are available, none is listed here.

Some excellent sources of information on *adult education* are:

Cross, K.P. *Accent on learning.* San Francisco: Jossey-Bass, 1976.

Gross, R. *The lifelong learner.* New York: Simon & Schuster, 1977.

Knowles, M. *Self-directed learning.* Chicago: Association Press/ Follett, 1975.

Knowles, M. *The adult learner: A neglected species* (2nd ed.). Houston, TX: Gulf, 1978.

Knowles, M. *The modern practice of adult education.* Chicago: Association Press/Follett, 1972.

Tough, A. *The adult's learning projects* (2nd ed.). San Diego, CA: Learning Concepts, 1979.

ANSWERS TO EXERCISE ON PAGES 34 and 35

1. Knowledge/rule learning and using
2. Physical/voice communicating
3. Physical/performing gross motor skills
4. Attitude/attitude learning
5. Physical/steering and guiding
6. Knowledge/making decisions
7. Attitude/attitude learning
8. Knowledge/detecting
9. Knowledge/rule learning and using
10. Physical/positioning movement and recalling procedures

ANSWERS TO EXERCISE ON PAGES 38 AND 39

1. Conduct a role play in which the learners can observe a worker being ridiculed publically and suffering the negative effects of such treatment.

2. Let the learners listen to tapes of actual airplane check-in messages. Then play tapes of improper ones and have the learners pick out the errors.

3. Provide a demonstration and then have the learners actually move the blocks.

4. As part of a presentation on esprit de corps, show visual aids of proper and improper civilian attire and have the learners comment on them. Then compare these to pictures of proper and improper battle dress and explain the need for proper dress and bearing.

5. Have the learners spend an hour trying to ride a unicycle, with an expert on hand to answer questions. Those learners who show the most progress can continue with advanced lessons. Those who have difficulty can be issued training wheels to help them to master the basic techniques.

6. Present several case studies that are based on actual occurrences of affirmative action that evolved out of otherwise routine labor disputes. Have the learners discuss the distinguishing points of each case.

7. Have a group of people who work together discuss the problems that are created in their job roles when someone else is late.

8. Show a training film in which pertinent symptoms are enacted as part of the drama, then reinforce recognition of those symptoms through the lesson material.

9. Have the learners restate the rules in their own words.

10. Demonstrate each procedure in a laboratory setting while explaining the reasons for each.

PART II
PREPARATION FOR TRAINING

Chapter 4
Getting Started

A trainer's first session with a group is a critical one. If it goes well, the way is paved for a succession of learning events in which maximum learning takes place.

When you have completed this chapter, you will be able to:

- make sure the physical learning facility is ready,
- properly prepare yourself for your role in the training event,
- present yourself so that the learners have confidence in your abilities as a trainer.

How many times have you heard the old saying about the importance of starting off on the right foot? Anyone who has marched with a band or military unit knows the significance of the phrase. Generally, something that starts right has a better chance of finishing right than something that starts badly. The importance of this concept to training is that to start properly may require far more work than does the actual training. If the first training session begins in the proper manner, the trainer feels good about it when it is all over; the learners feel good about the session, too; more learning probably has taken place; and the trainer has paved the way for the following sessions to be much smoother.

First impressions can be long lasting, and the first day of training sets the tone for the rest of the course. Fortunately, the fields of training and education, as well as life experience in general, have provided some widely accepted guidelines that can help you to start your first training session right.

BE PREPARED

The Scouts are right; although there are a few things worth doing that require little, if any, preparation, training is *not* one of them. A widely accepted ratio is three to one: for every hour of training presentation, you must spend *at least* three hours in preparation. Even the most experienced trainers have difficulty in achieving positive results from their efforts if they take short cuts in the preparation phase.

A number of things can be done in the name of preparation. Among them are:

- Making sure that the lesson outline is complete, detailed, and updated (see Chapter 5).
- Rehearsing until you are confident that you are ready.
- Anticipating learner questions and difficulties.
- Making sure that the room and all the resources you will need are available and ready.
- Checking out all audiovisual materials.
- Going back to source materials (text, experts, etc.) to review any areas of which you are uncertain.
- Mentally walking through the session from beginning to end, picturing in your mind everything that you expect to happen.
- Adding time to each element of the session to make sure that you have allocated enough time for everything and, conversely, that you have enough material to fill the time allocated, plus ten or fifteen percent.

It often is wise to be overprepared. Being overprepared means having additional materials, learner activities, questions, and so on, in case something takes less time than planned. If this does not prove to be necessary in your first session, it is likely to sometime (perhaps many times) before your career as a trainer is over.

TRAINING CHECK LIST

The training check list is an invaluable tool. Just as a pilot goes through an exhaustive check list before taking off in a 747 (no matter how many hours the pilot has logged), you should use your check list until it is second nature. A typical check list is shown in **Figure 2**. Never try to work without one.

Course/lesson: ―――――――――――――――――――――――

Date(s): ―――――――――――――――― Place: ―――――――――――――

Number of attendees: ――――――――― Number of rooms: ――――――――

Coordinator: ―――――――――――― Trainer/instructor: ―――――――――――

Item	Needed?	Done	Remarks
Workshop schedule/map			
Training room			
Learner work stations/layout			
Facilitator table/podium			
Public address system			
Chalkboard (chalk, erasers)			
Easels/tripods (paper, markers, tape)			
Screen			
Overhead projector (spare lamp)			
Other audiovisual devices			
Electrical outlets/extension cords			
Coffee breaks			
Meals			
Advance materials for attendees			
Facilitator materials (handouts, lesson plans, visuals, etc.)			
Learner materials (books, paper, name tags, pencils, etc.)			
Demonstration or practice equipment			
Recreation			
Lodging reservations			
Transportation arrangements			
Completion certificates			
Class evaluation forms			
Shipping cartons			
Other			

Figure 2. Training Session Check List

Workshop Schedule

The nature of the training session dictates the level of detail of the schedule. It may be all right merely to have an informal schedule that shows topic "A" in the morning, topic "B" in the afternoon, and so on. However, a detailed schedule does several things for you and for the learners:

1. It shows that the session has been well planned.
2. It helps to make sure that nothing has been overlooked (e.g., ending on time on Friday so that people can catch the last flight out).
3. It provides a planning tool for those who will be serving as facilitators. They will be better able to appear on time (and to stop on time, too).
4. It provides the time table by which learners will be living during the duration of the training. They want and deserve to know this information in advance.

If a map is needed to find one's way around the training site, be sure that it is included with the schedule.

Training Room

There are many details to attend to regarding the space in which you will be training. This is true whether the room is the corner of an empty storage room or a modern learning center. Even if someone else is responsible for setting up the room, and that fact has been made clear to you, pay attention to what is done. The trainer has the ultimate responsibility to cause everything to happen satisfactorily.

The best time to check things out is just before your session. This means far enough in advance to allow time to correct deficiencies, but close enough to zero hour that you can be confident that everything will still be ready when you return.

First, make sure that you have a room and that it is yours and only yours for the duration of the training. A perfectly good training session can be ruined if the trainer, followed by a line of long-faced participants, is tossed out of the training room because someone else claimed prior rights. This is one of the reasons why off-site facilities are nice, budget permitting.

Here are some other things to check regarding meeting rooms:

1. Personally inspect the room in advance.
2. Make sure that the size is right, not too small and not too large.
3. Make sure that the room is appropriate (e.g., a permanent theater arrangement is *not* appropriate if you need to break the learners into small groups).
4. Make sure that there is adequate ventilation.
5. Check to see that there are rest room facilities nearby.
6. Make sure that the air conditioning or heating is adequate.
7. Check to see if the lighting is sufficient and appropriate.

Learner Work Stations/Layout

Learner work stations should be comfortable (especially if the learners are expected to sit most of the day) and serve the purpose. A very flexible approach is to use tables that accommodate two or more people and separate chairs. This can be especially useful if you need to rearrange the setup at times to suit your needs. Ample room should be provided for the learners to lay out their work sheets, notes, texts, and other materials. Learning carrels may be required for training that has been individualized extensively. (These are individual desks that contain all the equipment—such as audiovisual aids—that is needed.) If the group will not be writing or taking notes, a circle of chairs may be the most effective arrangement. If the group primarily will be involved in experiential activities, tables and chairs may get in the way. In this case, you will want to make sure that the floor is clean and, probably, carpeted, so that participants can sit on the floor during discussion periods.

Figure 3 shows some common choices of layouts based on the approximate size of group.

Small-Group Arrangements

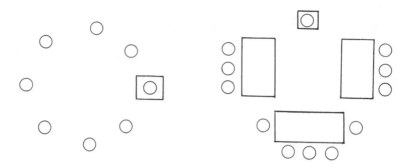

Medium-Group Arrangement

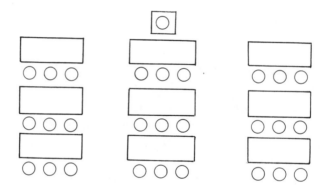

Large-Group Arrangement

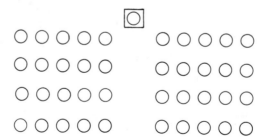

Figure 3. Typical Training Room Arrangements

- *Small* (up to twenty learners). A "U" shaped arrangement such as that shown in Figure 3 helps to make the learners feel part of a group and stimulates interaction. A circle offers the same possibility and lessens the focus on the trainer. The circle does not lend itself so well to the use of visual aids, but it is very effective for discussion groups in which the trainer takes a role that is equal to that of the other group members.
- *Medium* (twenty to forty learners). Rows, as shown in Figure 3, become more practical as the number of learners increases. This arrangement also lends itself to the use of tables. This is a more traditional classroom layout.
- *Large* (more than forty learners). Theater seating, as shown in Figure 3, is required when large numbers of learners are participating in one session. Consideration must be given to whether or not writing surfaces are required.

Facilitator Table/Podium

The trainer must have a place to do the "facilitating." This includes a place to keep handouts, audiovisual aids, projectors, and other materials, as well as a speaking platform if one is required. Some podiums have built-in public address systems, which may be required in larger rooms.

If the lights in the room will be dimmed (e.g., for a slide presentation), you may need lighting at the podium so that you can see your notes.

Easels/Tripods

These are a must if you plan to use newsprint, flip charts, and other large training aids. Of course, you also will need plenty of paper, felt-tipped markers, and masking tape (to post what is written).

Screen, Projectors, and Other Audiovisual Aids

Make sure that you have all the audiovisual devices that you need, that they are in good working order, and that a spare lamp (if not a spare projector) for each is on hand. (A more thorough discussion of the use of audiovisual aids appears in Chapter 6.)

Electrical Outlets/Extension Cords

Make sure that there is a working electrical outlet in a suitable location for each device you will be using. (This includes coffee pots as well as audiovisual aids.) For safety purposes, try to avoid having wires or cables stretched across places where people will be walking. (Also, it is always wise to carry a three-prong (grounded) extension cord and a plug to adapt it to two prongs as part of your training "Kit." Many new two-prong extension cords are polarized, that is, one prong is wider than the other. This reduces the chance of shock.

Coffee Breaks/Meals

Many training events include mid-morning and afternoon refreshments (coffee, tea, etc.). In some cases, meals are provided as well. These require more advance planning. Even if you are not responsible for making arrangements for food or beverages, be sure that the participants know what the arrangements are. If you are required to arrange for meals or refreshments, keep them as uncomplicated as possible without skimping on quality. Most conference facilities have a banquet manager whose job it is to help you with such arrangements. On the training end, sessions must be scheduled to accommodate breaks or meals. In many cases, this can be a critical element. Even when the participants are "on their own," there must at least be a coffee machine and a quick-food service handy. These days, many people prefer more healthful beverages, snacks, and meals.

Advance Materials for Attendees

At least two pieces of information must be provided in advance to learners who are to attend your training event: where it will be held and when. If the event is not to be conducted "in-house," you will need to include information on fees, eligibility requirements, travel and lodging arrangements, the weather, and other appropriate concerns. Beyond this you might want to enclose a letter of welcome, the schedule and map, advance reading matter, pretests, and so on. This also is the time to notify the learners of what, if anything other than themselves, they are to bring to the event.

Training Materials

When you complete the developmental phase of the training, you will have a check list of all the *facilitator* and *learner* materials required for the training session. These items should be added on or attached to the training session check list, along with the number of copies of each that is needed. If learners are going to accumulate many individual items, provide a binder or folder for them. Make arrangements for overnight storage of materials if it is not appropriate to leave them and any audiovisual equipment in the training room. Also make provision to transport in and out any demonstration or practice equipment or specially built aids. Finally, be sure that you have an adequate supply of name tags, pencils, blank paper, paper clips or staples, tape, and other such materials.

Recreation

It sometimes is appropriate to make available some facilities for recreation. This may be especially true in the case of highly intensive training sessions. If sports or exercise facilities will be available, let the participants know this before the session so that they can bring any clothing or equipment they might need. When they arrive at the training site, let them know where such facilities are to be found.

Lodging Reservations and Transportation Arrangements

When out-of-town participants will be arriving, or when the training event is off-site, someone must make hotel and transportation arrangements. If this is to be the responsibility of the participants, it should be made known well enough in advance for them to arange accommodations and travel. If the training site is to make arrangements for lodging, confirmations must be received far enough in advance that you can guarantee a certain number of guests to the hotel or lodging house. Advise the participants of when and where they should check in, and schedule check-in and registration at least one hour before the first meal or training session.

Airline transportation can be made easier by the use of a travel agent, at no cost to you. If it is difficult to obtain transportation to and from the airport and/or training site, advise the participants—in advance—of their options.

Completion Certificates

Completion-of-training certificates offer one means of recognizing achievement. They should be of good quality and tasteful. They can be distributed at the end of the training event or sent later. If the training is in-house, they can be distributed by the learners' boss to provide visibility for the achievement. It may be appropriate to notify the learners' personnel department if completion of the training has an effect on advancement or salary.

Evaluation Forms

This is an excellent means of obtaining feedback to the training staff. It also gives the learners a chance to respond to the training. (See Chapter 13 for more on this, including a sample evaluation form.)

Shipping Cartons

If the training event will culminate with the learners owning an enormous pile of materials, it might be appropriate to provide cartons in which they can take their materials home. If your budget is generous, you may want to arrange to ship or otherwise take care of bulky items.

PREPARING YOURSELF

How you, the trainer, look and feel is vital to the success of the training process. This includes your bearing, your actions, and the atmosphere you set for the learners.

Appearance is important. Your most casual, most comfortable clothes may be fine in a college classroom, but a neat appearance on the part of the trainer makes a positive contribution to the learning situation. Overdressing can be dysfunctional, too. The training situation (with some exceptions) is the same as the normal working environment of the learners.

A general rule to follow is: the more formal the training event, the more formal the attire. Some management training could call for a tailored suit; at a resort hotel, sports clothing might be appropriate; and at some types of training—generally more personal in focus—blue jeans are the order of the day. Another rule is to adopt the dress code of the organization for which you are providing the training. When in doubt, dress more formally. A jacket always can be removed if necessary. When you are wearing a tailored dress or a coat and tie, by the way, you need not remain stiff and formal.

Be conscious also of your *body language*. Good posture is important. Maintaining eye contact is a must. Be aware of what your body is communicating. Also, read what your participants are communicating to you.

Create a *comfortable atmosphere*. There is no reason why a warm, friendly atmosphere cannot prevail. Try to establish this at the outset and keep it that way. Enthusiasm and preparation pave the way for a comfortable learning situation in which the facilitator and the learners can enjoy as well as be serious about the learning process.

Relax. Do not get a death grip on the podium and freeze there for an hour. You are, literally, on stage, but as long as you maintain control, you can expect success. The best security blanket you can have is to be fully prepared. Just before beginning to speak, or any other time that you feel nervous, take two or three deep breaths. Slow down. Be more deliberate. This is a good way to avoid becoming tongue-tied, speaking in a squeak, or otherwise blithering in front of the group.

Several methods can be used to produce a state of relaxation. Books and articles on these techniques are readily available, and some have been recorded on cassette tape. Seminars on hypnosis and other relaxation techniques also are offered widely. A review of several of these methods identifies three main ingredients that are common to many of them:

- Breathe deeply, extending your abdomen as you breathe in, then pushing the air out.
- Turn your thoughts inward, focusing on your inner self and the state of relaxation, telling yourself to relax, slowly putting all external thoughts out of your mind.
- Start at either the top of your head or at your toes, take one muscle group at a time and tighten the muscles, then slowly relax them, working your way up (or down) your body until all your muscles are relaxed.

Some other things that you can do to prepare yourself are:

- Make it a habit to read body language. Several books are available on this subject.
- Practice giving your presentation in front of a mirror.
- Tape (videotape is terrific for this) yourself as you make your presentation. Then play it back and critique your performance.
- Observe old pros doing their thing as trainers and adopt their good habits.

IN THE BEGINNING

The first five minutes of your training session can be the most important. One approach is to jump right into the material. This is all right if the course is well underway. If it is your first time with the group, and especially if you are starting off the course, you might want to start with something more informal.

Here are some suggestions:

- Tell a joke. Not only must it be good, but it must be in good taste as well.
- Find out who the participants are and what their backgrounds are. This can be as simple as going around the room and having everyone respond.
- Use an activity called an "ice breaker." These are training tools that are structured experiences, i.e., the learners become involved in a preplanned activity with a specific purpose. In the case of an ice breaker, the purpose is to relax the group, have the members become acquainted with one another, and open them up to learning. (Chapter 11 contains more information about these.)

Get the learners involved immediately, whatever you do. And one last comment: *start on time.* The essential corollary to this is *end on time.*

SUMMARY

Being prepared and starting off well are unsurpassed in contributing to effective training. They also are closely related. Some key points related to this are:

1. Preparation, which includes rehearsing, should take several hours for every hour of training. This does not include the time required to design and develop the actual training materials.
2. Use a training check list to make certain that everything is physically ready for the training event.
3. Prepare yourself. Your bearing, appearance, and self-confidence are important.

4. The first five minutes of a training event can set the stage for the remainder of the event.

SELECTED REFERENCES

The following publications provide information on the subject of getting started—right:

Benson, H. *The relaxation response.* New York: Avon, 1975.

Davies, I.K. *Instructional technique.* New York: McGraw-Hill, 1981.

Davis, L.N. *Planning, conducting, and evaluating workshops.* San Diego, CA: Learning Concepts, 1974.

Fast, J. *Body language.* New York: Pocket Books, 1970.

Jongward, A. *Deep relaxation exercise.* Orinda, CA: TA Management Institute, 1977. (Cassette tape)

Newstrom, J.W., & Scannell, E.E. *Games trainers play.* New York: McGraw-Hill, 1980.

Nierenberg, G.I., & Calero, H.H. *How to read a person like a book.* New York: Pocket Books, 1971.

Randall, J.S. You and effective training: Part 1. *Training and Development Journal,* May, 1978, 10-14.

Walker, E.E. *Learn to relax.* Englewood Cliffs, NJ: Prentice-Hall, 1975.

Chapter 5
Preparing Learning Objectives
And Lesson Plans

A well-organized training session, based on clearly defined learning objectives, will give you the results you are striving for just about every time.

When you have completed this chapter, you will be able to:

- define learning objectives and their role in training,
- develop learning objectives,
- develop lesson plans.

Learning objectives and lesson plans have been mentioned repeatedly in previous chapters. Although their importance is stressed and they do require hard work, the requirements for developing them are based on common sense.

LEARNING OBJECTIVES

Learning objectives also have been called performance objectives and behavioral objectives. You also may have heard of the term "criterion-referenced instruction," which is based on performance objectives. It does not really matter what terminology is used; it is the concept that counts. The concept is that stating objectives for whatever project you might be involved in will do two things for you:

1. make sure that all your efforts are directed toward achieving *only* the *desired* results, and
2. tell you whether or not you have achieved them.

Looking back at Chapter 3, Learning Theory, you will note that there are three general kinds of things that you want learners to be able to do:

1. to know something (cognitive, or knowledge, learning);
2. to be able to do or perform something (psychomotor, or physical, skills);
3. to develop and exhibit a particular attitude about something (affective learning).

Here are examples of performance objectives for each of the three types of learning:

- State the eight prescribed safety precautions for operation of an acetylene torch (knowledge objective).
- Weld two pieces of one-quarter-inch steel together (psychomotor skill).
- Demonstrate how to convince an irate customer that you are genuinely concerned about his problem (affective objective).

The key is to use *action* words, denoting something that can be measured and/or observed. For example, understanding is extremely difficult to measure. The words "state," "show," and "solve," on the other hand, are precise and measurable.

Another key is to develop only those objectives that are directly relevant to the training at hand. When it is all over, just what do you want the learners to know and to be able to do? This is what the objectives should state. The training should accomplish these and only these objectives.

The Three-Part Objective

To make objectives even more useful, they can be divided into three parts. The first part is the performance, which is what we have discussed. The second part is the *condition* under which the performance is to be attained. The third is the *standard* of performance. Here are the welding objectives stated previously, with conditions and standards added. Note that the new elements are stated just as precisely as the performance.

Performance: State the eight prescribed safety precau-
tions for operation of an acetylene torch,
Condition: from memory,
Standard: without error.
Performance: Weld two pieces of one-quarter-inch steel
together,
Condition: using a standard welding rig and no assis-
tance from the instructor,
Standard: in a straight line with no flaws.

There is no doubt about what is expected when objectives are complete and precise.

Good and Bad Examples

Here are some examples of how not to write the performance
portion of learning objectives. Each is followed by an
acceptable rendition. Note the following characteristics,
which are absent from the bad examples and present in the
good ones:

- There is no doubt on the part of the learner about
what is required.
- Action is intended for the learner's (performer's)
benefit, not the trainer's or anyone else's.
- Performance can be measured; after an attempt is
made, it is possible to tell clearly whether or not the
objective has been achieved.
- Clear, precise, action words are used.

Example #1

Bad: Know when to use the inland rules of the road in a
sailing vessel.
Good: State the conditions under which the inland rules of
the road apply to a sailing vessel.

The learner may know all the rules, but would not
otherwise be able to show that he or she knew when to use
them. If measurable action cannot be performed, have the
learner explain when (how, etc.) it would be performed and
under what conditions.

Example #2

Bad: Show how to start a payroll program on the computer.

Good: Using the proper procedures, initiate a payroll program run on the computer system.

Show is an action word, but you can "show" by drawing a picture, using your hands, or other means. You want the learner to physically manipulate the computer, so say it.

Example #3

Bad: Understand the meaning of symbiosis.

Good: Identify the three major types of symbiosis and state the primary differences between them.

"Understand" is one of the words that is most often misused in writing objectives. It is too indefinite to be measured.

Example #4

Bad: Appreciate the value of safety goggles.

Good: List three reasons for wearing safety goggles while operating a metal lathe (knowledge skill) and demonstrate how to wear safety goggles properly while operating a metal lathe (performance skill).

The words "appreciate" and "value" also are too vague to be measured.

EXERCISE

Rewrite the following (poorly worded) objectives, using action words and making them as clear as possible. Make you own assumptions and add information wherever you believe it will help. After finishing the performance segments, add conditions and standards. Make up your own data (so long as it is precise and measurable) to complete the three parts. The important thing is technique. Some examples of acceptable versions are found at the end of this chapter.

1. Understand the principles of learning given in this book.

2. Operate a duplicating machine for nonstandard jobs.

3. Talk about how to properly use an overhead projector.

4. Show appreciation for the value of being prepared as a trainer.

LESSON PLANS

Just as a learning objective serves as a road map and a check to see if learning is accomplished, the lesson plan guides the trainer through the process (training event) that causes the learning to occur. You can think of a lesson plan as a combination of speaker's notes, recipe, and script. It is an outline of everything that is to happen during the training event. In the case of individualized instruction, the lesson plan serves as the lesson specification from which the computerized or programmed text is derived.

One of the requirements for being prepared is to have a lesson plan. Even if the training is a thirty-minute presentation that is to be delivered but once, a plan is essential.

Elements of a Lesson

A lesson plan format is shown in Figure 4. It consists of several parts. The administrative part of the plan is found in part a. These items are helpful to both the facilitator and the learner in making the most of the lesson.

Course title: _____

Lesson title: _____

Lesson number: _____ Latest revision date: _____

Learning objectives:

Target audience/job classification:

Prerequisites:

Student preparation:

Student materials:

Instructor materials/preparation:

References:

Evaluation and follow-up/outside assignments:

Lesson length:

Comments:

Figure 4a. Lesson Plan: General Lesson Information

Course: _____ Time: _____

Lesson: _____

Lesson Outline	Comments, References, Hand-outs, Visual Aids
This includes the introduction to the lesson, which always includes making sure that the learners know the objectives; the material to be presented (in outline form); the summary of key points; and all learner activities, including questions for the trainer to ask.	These items are placed at the appropriate points to indicate where they are to occur during the lesson.

Figure 4b. Lesson Plan: Lesson Outline/Activities

Perhaps the most important element of the lesson is the listing of objectives. The next element is the outline. You begin this by listing the main points, then adding until you have enough to make sure that everything is covered during the lesson. *Do not rely on your memory.* Finally, reorganize the material as necessary to make sure that it flows smoothly and logically.

The complete outline has three parts: a beginning, a middle, and an end. The beginning states the objectives and describes what material is to be covered and how it is going to be done. This also may include any activities for setting the stage for the learning that is to take place, e.g., background material, brief review of material covered previously, definitions.

The middle of the outline is all the material that must be covered in order for each learner to be able to accomplish the learning objectives. This usually is a point-by-point, logical sequence from the beginning of the prescribed subject matter to the end.

The end includes a summary of key points, highlighting the presentation. Remember the old saying: Tell them what you're going to tell them, tell them, and then tell them what you told them.

The next step is to take care of the element found in the right-hand column of the plan (Figure 4b.). At this point, you plan just what you are going to do; you mentally walk through the lesson several times and make it come to life on paper. If you develop visual aids to emphasize points, you will want to make notes about where to use them during the lesson. You may also think of anecdotes to relate and questions to ask, tests to give and handouts to distribute, references to cite, and things for the learners to do.

Once you have completed a lesson plan, think of it as a dynamic entity. Every time you use it, try to find ways to improve it. Make notes right on the form as you go through the lesson. You rarely can have too much detail or too many notes about what to do on a lesson plan. The exception is if you proceed to read the plan verbatim to the learners. The lesson plan is *your* tool—before the lesson to help you to be prepared, during the lesson in order to help you to facilitate a successful learning process, and after the lesson to help you to evaluate whether or not you (and the learners) made it.

Training-Course Outline

If your training event consists of several lessons and related events, it is advisable to develop a training-course outline. This document is a combination of selected information about the training event and a catalog of items in the event. The more individual elements of training there are, the more elaborate it should be. The information required is similar to that in part a of Figure 4. Some information to be included is:

- course/event title and number,
- major objectives,
- target audience/job classification,
- brief description,
- planned length,
- prerequisites,

- special requirements/equipment,
- list of individual events.

Lesson-Plan Numbering Scheme

A numbering scheme for training materials *may* be more trouble than it is worth, unless you have more than a few materials and/or you use them quite often. In these cases, it can be very worthwhile. If more than one person uses the material, a numbering scheme can be even more valuable. Such a scheme need not be elaborate. The following is a sample of one that has been used successfully. Elements that are not needed can be eliminated.

XXXXX-Y11. XXXXX is a five-character, alphabetical abbreviation of the course; Y is an alphabetical character designating the module (for large courses that are divided into modules); and 11 is a two-digit number designating the lesson number.

For example, TRATR-L04 might be a train-the-trainer course (TRATR) in which L is the module covering lesson-plan preparation and 04 denotes the fourth lesson in the module.

An additional character can be added to the Y11 to identify the type of lesson, such as classroom, laboratory, field trip, programmed instruction, and so on.

Visual aids, learner handouts, assignments, and tests also can be cataloged (if you have very many of them) by adding another character group, for example:

XXXXX-Y11-A22. A is an alphabetical character designating a handout, visual aid, test, or assignment, and 22 is the sequential number of the handout or other item.

To continue the previous example, TRATR-L04-T10 would indicate the tenth transparency to be used in the course.

Clearly labeled training materials can take the guesswork out of training-event preparation and presentation.

A Sample Lesson Plan

A sample (abbreviated) lesson plan is shown in Figure 5. It shows the level of detail and variety of information that is needed in this important training tool. This particular lesson is a classroom presentation that is designed to introduce learners to a computer system that they soon will be learning to operate. The knowledge that they gain will be reinforced in the next lesson, which will be a demonstration of the system. Thus, this is an introductory, overview lesson.

Course title: Computer-System Operator Course

Lesson title: Computer-System Introduction

Lesson number: SYSOP-01   Latest revision date: 5/8/82

Learning objectives: Name major uses of the system
Identify who is responsible for various operations
Name major components of the system

Target audience/job classification: All clerical and management personnel; potential system operators

Prerequisites: none

Student preparation: none

Student materials: brochure, handout set for this lesson

Instructor materials/preparation:
1. visual-aid set for this presentation
2. overhead projector and screen

References: System-user manual; standard accounting-practices manual

Evaluation and follow-up/outside assignments:
review operator manual (potential operators only)

Lesson length: thirty minutes

Comments: This lesson can be used on a stand-alone basis to familiarize nonoperators with the system.

Figure 5a. Sample Lesson Plan: General Lesson Information

Lesson: Computer-System Introduction   **Time:**   Thirty minutes

Lesson Outline	Comments, References, Handouts, Visual Aids
A. Welcome learners	
1. point out that some will be present only for the first two hours	
B. State objectives	T01
1. major uses	
2. responsibilities	
3. components	
C. Overview	
1. background material	
2. nomenclature	
3. knowledge of total system	
4. following lessons will look at details	
D. Major components	T02
1. input devices	H01 (handout)
a. user terminals (CRTs)	T03
b. magnetic tapes	T04
2. processor/memory	T05
3. mass storage devices	T06
4. output devices	T07
E. Responsibilities	T08
1. supervisors	
2. operators	T09
3. service technicians	
4. users	
etc.	

Figure 5b. Sample Lesson Plan: Lesson Outline/Activities

SUMMARY

Learning objectives provide the criteria on which training is designed, developed, conducted, and evaluated. They define the performance that is expected from the learner. Complete objectives also state standards of performance and conditions under which performance is to be accomplished. Learning objectives must be:

- defined with action words,
- precise,
- measurable.

Just as learning objectives guide the overall training toward the desired results, lesson plans provide detailed guidelines (including specific objectives) for each block of training in the overall training event. Containing a beginning (objectives, materials covered, how), a middle (point-by-point sequence), and an end (summary), the lesson plan must contain all that must be done for and during the lesson.

SELECTED REFERENCES

References related to learning objectives, lessons, and developing training materials in general can be grouped into three categories: those from education, those from the military establishment, and those from the training and development field. Most of the references that follow are in the last group. Some good military materials are available from the Government Printing Office, Washington, D.C. 20402, and the National Technical Information Service (NTIS), 5285 Port Royal Road, Springfield, Virginia 22161.

Briggs, L.J. (Ed.). *Instructional design.* Englewood Cliffs, NJ: Educational Technology Publications, 1977.

Davies, I. *Instructional technique.* New York: McGraw-Hill, 1981.

Davis, L.N. *Planning, conducting, and evaluating workshops.* San Diego, CA: Learning Concepts, 1974.

Fleming, M., & Levie, W.H. *Instructional message design.* Englewood Cliffs, NJ: Educational Technology Publications, 1978.

Kapfer, M.B. (Ed.). *Behavioral objectives in curriculum development.* Englewood Cliffs, NJ: Educational Technology Publications, 1971.

Mager, R.F., & Beach, K.M., Jr. *Developing vocational instruction.* Belmont, CA: Fearon, 1967.

Mager, R.F. *Preparing instructional objectives* (2nd ed.). Belmont, CA: Fearon, 1975.

O'Neil, H.F., Jr. (Ed.). *Procedures for instructional systems development.* New York: Academic Press, 1979.

ANSWERS TO EXERCISE ON PAGES 66 AND 67

1. Performance: State at least five principles of learning discussed in Chapter 3 of this book,
   Condition: from memory,
   Standard: in words closely approximating those in the book.

2. Performance: Using a duplicating machine, make copies using the following special features:
   a. reduced size,
   b. oversized copy,
   c. multiple copies,
   Condition: using instructions available at the machine,
   Standard: on the first attempt.

3. Performance: List the rules for proper use of an overhead projector,
   Condition: from memory,
   Standard: including correctly listing at least three of the rules given in Chapter 5 of this book.

4. Performance: Prepare a lesson guide for delivering a classroom presentation on the benefits of trainer preparedness,
   Condition: within three working days,
   Standard: containing all the information required in Figure 5.

Chapter 6
Using Audiovisual Aids

Instructional media provide powerful tools for making the training process more effective. Knowing when and how to use them will make you a better trainer.

When you have completed this chapter, you will be able to:

- identify the most common instructional media,
- identify the basic requirements for visual aids,
- properly use the most common visual aids.

Audiovisual aids are important tools for the trainer. They accomplish a lot of things, such as:

- highlighting key points,
- repeating material in a different way,
- providing a common focal point for the learners,
- gaining the attention of the learners,
- adding variety,
- serving as the next best thing to actually demonstrating a machine or piece of equipment,
- keeping the trainer on track.

There are two aspects of using audiovisual media: selecting the appropriate media and using it. Because the requirements of each course are unique, this chapter primarily will discuss the latter aspect. Because the overhead projector is the most widely used visual aid, it will be discussed in detail. The United States (not to mention a growing portion of the rest of the world) is a media-oriented society. We are exposed to vast amounts of television, billboards, magazines, and pictures and symbols from a wide variety of sources. Training and education can take advantage of this fact to reach a large part of our media-oriented society.

TYPES OF INSTRUCTIONAL MEDIA

Instructional media comprise a vast subject. As in other branches of technology today, many people have become experts in small, narrowly defined segments of media, such as video or computer-assisted instruction. There are many categories of media, ranging from the simple to the highly sophisticated. Some of them are as follows:

- still visuals include those drawn on chalkboard or newsprint; posters and handouts; those projected from overhead projectors, slide projectors, or film-strip projectors; and still images from a computer-generated video-display terminal.

- audio can be from recordings such as cassette or reel-to-reel tape or from phonograph records.

- motion visuals include motion pictures; video, including live video and videotape; automated projections from slide projectors; videodisc; and motion images from a computer-generated video-display terminal.

- still visuals with sound can be composed of various combinations such as a slide projector and cassette tape or a film strip with a record or tape.

- moving visuals with sound can be composed of various combinations such as sound motion pictures or videotape with recorded sound.

- combinations include such multimedia presentations as sound motion pictures with two or more thirty-five millimeter slide projectors alongside.

As one progresses from still visuals to the more complicated combinations of media, ease of use decreases and flexibility, preparation time, and costs increase.

Some systems, such as computer-assisted instructional terminals interfaced with videodisc under computer control, essentially include "all of the above." CAI terminals can have graphic capability, and the videodisc can include motion pictures and videotape with sound, along with slides. These highly complex training systems, featuring advanced audiovisual capabilities, are gaining increasingly greater acceptance in the training field.

The most commonly used instructional aids are transparencies used with overhead projectors, thirty-five millimeter slides and projectors (also used with audio cassette tapes), film strips (with or without sound), motion pictures, and videotape. However, you will find that the more simple—but widely used—items such as the chalkboard, newsprint, posters, and handouts are indispensable.

RULES FOR USING VISUAL AIDS

Visual aids are tools. They can simplify instruction and help you to achieve the results you are after. They will not do it for you, however. These general rules are the result of experience:

1. Media must be *planned* and *selected* well in *advance.* The more sophisticated it is, the more critical it is to check it out in advance.
2. Visual aids should be in compliance with the basic principles of adult education; that is, they should be *realistic, relevant,* and *related* to the learning objectives.
3. Keep visuals *simple* and *uncluttered* so that all members of the audience can follow them.
4. Use *good taste.* Trainers have been known to sneak the playperson of the month into their visuals, but the risk of offending someone this way is great.
5. Maintain a *consistent format,* rather than mixing several different ones. A horizontal format is best because most people are accustomed to reading horizontal lines.
6. *Review* all visuals *thoroughly* before using them.

For written visuals, these are additional rules:[2]
1. Do not use more than four or five words per line.
2. Do not have more than three vertical columns.
3. Do not use vertical dividing lines; use space.
4. Do condense information.
5. Do use large symbols and abbreviations.
6. Do eliminate every unnecessary word or figure.
7. Do design the material so that it can be read easily from the back row of the audience.
8. Do remember that the larger the symbol, the greater will be its visual impact.

WHEN TO USE WHAT

Media selection, in which several relevant factors are compared along with a lengthy array of potential media, can become quite a detailed process. Fortunately, several methods are available to help to simplify the job somewhat. One, for example, provides flow charts that lead you through the process to the appropriate medium, or—as is often the case—media (there is not always just one that is significantly better than the others).[3] Several factors are involved, some key ones being the nature of the learning objectives, the size of the learner group, and the availability of resources. Generally, the larger the size of the group, the more formal the media required. Another general practice is to attempt to stimulate as many of the audience's senses as practicable.

If you will not be using a piece of audiovisual equipment regularly, it may be a good idea to rent it when you do need it. Renting also allows you to experiment with various types of equipment and saves you the trouble of transporting equipment from one location to a distant one.

If you do decide to purchase audiovisual equipment, read the product warranty carefully, determine the equip-

---

[2]From "Audiovisuals and the Training Process" by Kevin O'Sullivan, in *Training and Development Handbook*, edited by Robert L. Craig. Copyright © 1976 by McGraw-Hill, Inc. Used with the permission of McGraw-Hill Book Company.

[3]Ronald H. Anderson, *Selecting and Developing Media for Instruction.* New York: Van Nostrand Reinhold, 1976.

ment's compatibility with other equipment, and find out whether certified repair service is available in your area. When in doubt, consult with people who actually use such equipment and take advantage of any loan programs offered by distributors.

Some general rules are:

1. Use *audio* to help reduce facilitator involvement; this also provides variety from hearing the trainer's voice so much.

2. *Slides, transparencies,* and *film* work well when the facilitator is an integral part of the learning environment.

3. *Video, videodiscs,* and *computers* work well when the learner is more in control of the learning process.

Many other media exist (filmstrips, teaching machines, microfilm, opaque projectors), but are used less commonly by trainers.

THE OVERHEAD PROJECTOR: THE INSTRUCTOR'S HELPER

The medium that you probably will use most often is the overhead projector. This device has been around for a long time and for good reasons: it is inexpensive, is flexible in its applications, is adaptable to many situations, is easy to use, does not require a darkened room, and is reliable. Generally, you will be using transparencies (also called vugraphs) with the overhead projector. The following hints will help in using this machine.

Make sure that the machine is operable before you start the session. Check to see that you have (a) a spare lamp; (b) the glass and lens wiped off; and (c) adjusted the machine properly (use a test transparency).

Everyone in the room should be able to see the screen clearly and read the projected image without strain. Avoid distortion.

Have your transparencies in the proper order and turned the right way. You should not have to turn them to put them on the machine.

Go through the motions that you would use in the session. Set the stack of transparencies in the most advantageous position. You don't want to have to do a juggling act as part of your presentation.

Turn off the projector any time that you do not have a transparency about which you are speaking. If the visual is not the current focus of attention, turn it off, even if you intend eventually to refer back to it. Never leave the projector on without a visual aid.

Use the pointer technique. Just put the tip of a pen or pencil directly on the transparency item that you want to highlight and the image will be projected on the screen. An alternative is to use a long pointer and point directly to the screen. Either way, pointing helps to focus the learners' attention. You also can highlight portions of transparencies with a special (washable) marking pen.

Use overlays. You can build a picture or add key points by folding over pieces of transparency as you move along through your material.

If you discover a problem with a transparency, such as blurred, erroneous material or copy that is too busy, make a note immediately. Then be creative and find a way to get around the problem in the current session.

Never go into the training room without having inspected each visual, even if you used it only yesterday. Gremlins have a way of creeping into training materials.

Keep visuals in order as you use them. It takes no more time and it keeps you organized and under control. You will be glad that you did.

Be conscious of where you are standing, because it is easy to block the view of people on one side of the room or the other. *The pointer technique* is one way to avoid this problem.

Making Transparencies

Elaborate transparencies—four color, photographs, award-winning graphics, animated cartoon characters, etc.—are available for use with an overhead projector. Some are intricate overlays that build a story as you go along. They add immensely to the professional appearance of a training session—and also to the cost. One alternative is to have professionally prepared 8½" x 11" art boards professionally drawn and mechanically lettered and to have the transparency made in black and white from these. If a special transparency machine is not available, you can use some duplicating machines that accept the transparent acetate material and make adequate transparencies. Using this technique allows you to duplicate items directly from existing materials, which can be useful.

Another alternative is to use a typewriter to make the 8½" by 11" masters. These are more difficult to see, but will do the job. The final alternative is to create your own handwritten transparencies, either before the event or on the spot. A clean piece of clear acetate and a special marking pen will allow you to do this quite easily.

SLIDE PROJECTORS

Slide projectors, popular for home use as well as in training facilities, are widely used as audiovisuals aids. Extensive off-the-shelf slide programs are readily available. The use of color and photographs along with graphics is made possible with these easily operated devices. Programs can be upgraded with little difficulty, and sound (such as cassette tape) can be played simultaneously. The same rules that apply to overhead transparency graphics also apply to slides. The two drawbacks to this medium are that the equipment and production costs are more expensive than are transparencies and that the room generally must be darkened to show slides.

A variety of slide projectors are available. The differences generally are in the receptacles that hold the slides (thirty-five millimeter is the most common size) and those that feed them into the projector.

Slides must be prearranged in the proper order in the tray, cube, or other holding device for use in the slide projector. You usually will want to run through your presentation prior to the training session to make sure that the slides are arranged properly (not sideways, upside down, or backwards). Unless you have random-access capability, have duplicates of those slides to which you want to refer back.

Slide projectors can be simple or they can include such capabilities as multiple projectors; fade-in, fade-out devices; programmers that automatically advance the slide when cued by a signal; sound that is synchronized to play along with the images; and random access. The use of these, of course, requires greater skill, preparation, and investment.

USING OTHER VISUAL AIDS

The original classroom visual aid is the chalkboard. The board should be clean and there should be plenty of spare chalk available, as well as an eraser. The chalkboard is a versatile, tried-and-true means of highlighting, illustrating, listing main points, providing a history of the discussion, and otherwise delivering a visual message.

If you prefer, an easel or tripod with a large pad of newsprint and a felt-tipped marker can be used in a similar way. In addition, the newsprint sheets can be retained and taped to the wall for reference. This is especially handy when you need to refer to material days or weeks later. There also are boards tht one writes on with washable markers. These can be wiped off and used in the same way as a chalkboard. With these media, different colors of chalk or markers can be used to make distinctions, show emphasis, or chart time lines.

Other media that you might want to use from time to time are:

- *Video tape:* this requires special equipment and expertise.
- *Video disc:* rapidly gaining in popularity, partly because of the potential interface with computers.
- *Computer-assisted instruction* (CAI): this also requires special equipment and expertise.
- *Simulators:* this usually is expensive.

Generally, these all require more advanced knowledge and experience in their use.

Screens

Although you do not need to use a screen with visual aids (a clean, white or near-white wall will do), a screen that is of the right texture and that is well placed will make your use of visuals much more effective. Mat-white screens provide the best image when you are using the overhead projector. Glass-beaded and silver lenticular screens work well with film and color.

Figure 6 shows how to set up a projector and screen for optimum viewing. It also gives a formula for determining the image size that is required.

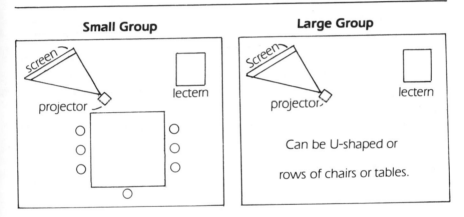

Small Group   **Large Group**

lectern   lectern

projector   projector

Can be U-shaped or

rows of chairs or tables.

(Having the screen in a corner allows all to view it easily.)

The 2-and-6-Rule for Proper Screen Size

The size of the screen (and image) should be as near this size as possible:

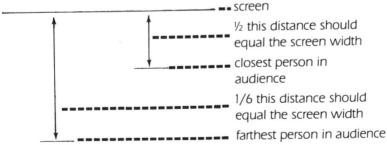

screen

½ this distance should equal the screen width

closest person in audience

1/6 this distance should equal the screen width

farthest person in audience

Figure 6. How To Place a Projector Screen

EXERCISES

1. See if you can find five things that are wrong with the visual display found in Figure 7. The answers are listed at the end of this chapter.

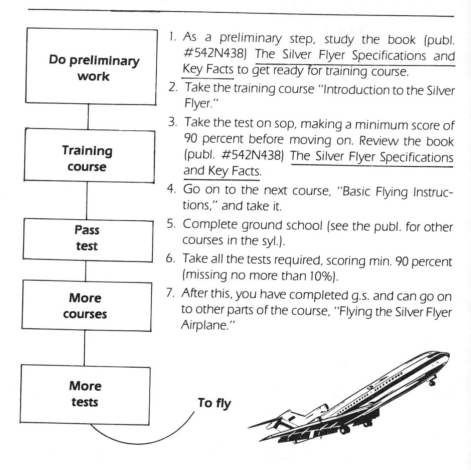

	1. As a preliminary step, study the book (publ. #542N438) *The Silver Flyer Specifications and Key Facts* to get ready for training course.
Do preliminary work	2. Take the training course "Introduction to the Silver Flyer."
	3. Take the test on sop, making a minimum score of 90 percent before moving on. Review the book (publ. #542N438) *The Silver Flyer Specifications and Key Facts.*
Training course	4. Go on to the next course, "Basic Flying Instructions," and take it.
	5. Complete ground school (see the publ. for other courses in the syl.).
Pass test	6. Take all the tests required, scoring min. 90 percent (missing no more than 10%).
More courses	7. After this, you have completed g.s. and can go on to other parts of the course, "Flying the Silver Flyer Airplane."
More tests **To fly**	

8. Practice flying in the actual aircraft.

Note: This visual is being used to illustrate the point that FAA safety regulations require that students learning to fly the Silver Flyer Aircarft must complete ground school and be certified by the FAA before taking airborne lessons.

Figure 7. Sample Visual Aid: How To Fly An Airplane

2. Have someone demonstrate to you how to use the following:

    a. an overhead projector

    b. a slide projector

    While you are at it, practice removing and replacing the lamps.

3. Put together an emergency kit consisting of a box of chalk (chalk disappears!), a collapsible pointer, a roll of masking tape, a few pieces of transparency material, markers suitable for writing on the transparencies, felt-tipped markers for writing on newsprint, blank paper, an extension cord, a flashlight, and pencils. (You might want to add a bottle of aspirin.) A spare set of instructor lesson plans also can come in handy on occasion. Experience will help you to assemble a complete set of indispensible emergency training items.

SUMMARY

Audiovisual aids highlight, reinforce, and further the learning process. A wide variety of choices is available, ranging from a computerized random-access system to a piece of chalk. The methods to be used will depend on many factors, including cost, the nature of the training, the size of the group, the physical facilities available, and so on.

Some of the key points from this chapter are:

1. The overhead projector probably is the most commonly used and most versatile audiovisual medium.

2. Follow the suggested guidelines for using any equipment and practice ahead of time.

3. Keep your media and your materials organized.

SELECTED REFERENCES

There are many periodicals in the human resource development and audiovisual fields in which articles and general information can be found. Check your organization's training resources, call a manufacturer or distributor of materials and equipment, or go to the library to find them as well as much other information.

The following also are excellent references. Many of them have excellent bibliographies.

Anderson, R.H. *Selecting and developing media for instruction.* New York: Van Nostrand Reinhold, 1976.

Association for Educational Communications and Technology. *Selecting media for learning.* Washington, DC: Author, 1974.

Davidson, A.R. Selecting an appropriate video system. In J.E. Jones & J.W. Pfeiffer (Eds.), *The 1979 annual handbook for group facilitators.* San Diego, CA: University Associates, 1979.

Davies, I.K. *Instructional technique.* New York: McGraw-Hill, 1981. (Chapter 10 is about audiovisual aids.)

Kemp, J. *Planning and producing audio visual materials* (3rd ed.). New York: Crowell, 1975.

O'Sullivan, K. Audiovisuals and the training process. In R.L. Craig (Ed.), *Training and development handbook* (2nd ed.). New York: McGraw-Hill, 1976.

ANSWERS TO EXERCISE 1 ON PAGE 86

1. Too much material; too many points made.
2. Does not convey the full message (why is note at bottom necessary?).
3. Repeats full titles of documents (unnecessary).
4. Uses undefined abbreviations (publ., sop, syl., g.s.).
5. Mixes words and symbols. This adds confusion.
6. Too many words.
7. Misleading title.
8. Key points not highlighted.

PART III
IMPLEMENTATION OF TRAINING

Chapter 7
Interpersonal Communication

Interpersonal communication is a closed-loop, two-way process involving sender, receiver, message, and means of transmittal. Success in training is directly proportional to success in communicating.

When you have completed this chapter, you will be able to:

- state the functions of the components of the communication system and the importance and role of each,
- identify and use positive communication patterns,
- identify and use nonverbal communication techniques.

A VITAL TOOL

A scientific law states that for every action, there must be an opposite and equal reaction. Effective communication complies with this principle. The fact that most communication is not scientific, however, causes unequal and undesired reactions more often than should be the case.

Communication is the trainer's most vital tool. This communication may range from a monologue to a multimedia event using some speech, symbols in the form of audiovisual aids, and discussion and feedback from the learners.

The element of communication is present in many of the techniques discussed in this book. Chapter 6 (audiovisual

91

aids), Chapter 8 (active listening), Chapter 9 (transactional analysis), and Chapter 11 (questioning) all deal directly with how to communicate.

Our first concern in this chapter is with oral communication. The most important communication we achieve is through the spoken word. Nonverbal communication also fulfills an important role in interpersonal relations. This form of communication is addressed later in the chapter.

THE COMMUNICATION PROCESS

One general model applies to all the methods of communication. The ingredients of this model are:
- sender,
- receiver,
- message,
- channel.

This is shown in Figure 8. The sender begins the process. The receiver ultimately becomes a sender, too, because of the requirement to acknowledge the message.

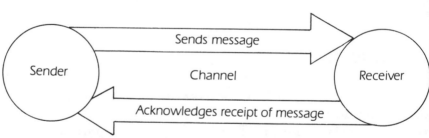

Figure 8. A Model of The Communication Process

The message may be anything ranging from a simple "Hi" to instructions for landing a spacecraft on the moon; from something as positive as an elaborate, hand-crafted Valentine card to failure to speak to an acquaintance passed on the street. The channel is the means by (or through) which the message is conveyed between the two (or more) parties. Examples of channels are telephone lines, faces, voices, written materials, drum beats, puffs of smoke, and so on.

Communication literally is a two-way process. Anything less is not communication. Even when two-way, the complete process is a closed loop, ending with the positive feedback that understanding has been achieved. Any time that two or more people are together, communication of some kind occurs—either verbally; visually, through symbols, pictures, and so on; through actions such as showing, pointing, gesturing, or demonstrating; through the use of facial expression and bodily position; and sometimes through what does *not* occur. The pyramid in Figure 9 shows some specific communication media.

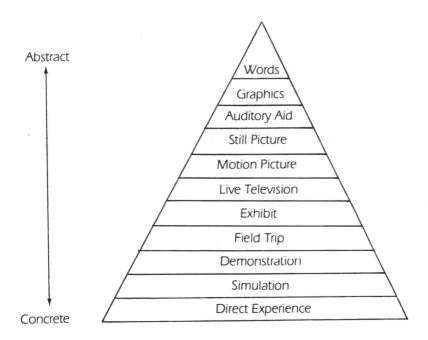

From "Training Aids" by Louis S. Goodman, in *Training and Development Handbook* (1st ed.), edited by Robert L. Craig and Lester R. Bittel. Copyright © 1967 by McGraw-Hill, Inc. Used with the permission of McGraw-Hill Book Company.

Figure 9. The Communication Pyramid

Telling is not communicating—and it is not training, either. Everything within the environment in which communication is trying to happen has an effect on the process. In many situations, you can control only a few of the variables. In an instructional setting, you have the opportunity to control many of the ones that count.

VERBAL COMMUNICATION

It has been said that the ability to communicate through language is what sets the human species apart from all others. Unfortunately, not all people have equal skill in communicating. You can, however, increase your communication skills by learning certain principles and practicing.

Simplicity is a primary key to effective communication. Simple, clear language usually is all that is required, and it can keep you out of trouble. Jargon can get you into trouble, unless it is terminology that both you and your listeners understand well. You can build rapport if you use terms, especially technical ones, with which the group is familiar, but this must be handled carefully and correctly. Few learners will be insulted if you use simple, precise words and sentences. After all, your intention is to communicate, not to intimidate or to impress.

EXERCISE

Rewrite the two paragraphs below, making them as much shorter as possible and using simpler words. Examples of more concise versions are found at the end of this chapter.

1. Due to the requirement to maximize human assets, which are yet in short supply in some of the more critical skill areas, this new company policy is being actualized. All personnel in the employ of this company are subject to this policy and must be cognizant of it. The policy is as follows: a person believed to be in a state of inebriation or showing signs attributable to any state of intoxication shall be removed from active employee status (i.e., not allowed to

continue working, but not yet terminated) until such time as an investigation can be accomplished. Such investigation shall be commenced as soon as possible after the alleged offense and concluded, with a formal report (to include recommendations), no later than forty-eight hours after the offense. The person to conduct the investigation shall be in management and shall be the supervisor of the alleged offender.

2. For purposes of this memorandum, an employee is defined as any person who works for and receives wages for the minimal time of thirty hours during each successive week and is thus considered to be a person of full-time employment. Henceforth, a new policy of the company is that any person to whom the definition above is applicable shall maximize productive time on the job by not commencing the work day at any time other than the normal, officially mandated starting time for work for that person's department. Persons who desire to make exceptions will not be accommodated.

Tips for Good Verbal Communication

Here are some tips to help you to increase your verbal training skills. You will note that the list refers to eliminating bad habits as well as to reinforcing good ones.

- *Eliminate* "er" and "ah" from your vocabulary.
- *Use illustrations freely,* but be sure that the learners can relate to them.
- *Avoid long monologues;* in fact, avoid all monologues, if possible. Make your presentation as natural as possible and break up your speaking with other activities.
- *Do not appear to be reading aloud.* For this purpose, an outline is better than a complete script, and being prepared is critical.
- *Avoid sexism.* It is easy to do when you try.
- *Speak up.* Do not talk to the wall, to your knees, or to your co-trainers. Vary your pitch, but always be distinct.

- *Keep water handy.* You may need it (but water only).
- *Monitor your velocity.* This may take some practice, but be careful of speaking too rapidly or too slowly.
- *Establish eye contact* with the learners. They are more apt to listen and to respond if they perceive that you are speaking to them.
- *Use correct grammar.* There is no reason to talk down to any audience.
- *Avoid the use of slang.* Occasionally, it may be appropriate for comic relief; but as a rule, clear, precise, simple language is best.
- *Use appropriate gestures and visual aids* to accentuate what you are saying.

The following are several traits to cultivate and demonstrate.

- *Empathy.* If you are having trouble communicating with a particular individual, try to put yourself in that person's shoes. Do it with an open mind, and you probably will discover why you have been unsuccessful in communicating.
- *Respect.* A little awareness and genuine kindness go a long way.
- *Desire* to facilitate the learners' acquisition of the knowledge and skills that *they* desire.

Perception

Perception plays an important role in communication. It can help immensely and it can devastate the most sincere effort to communicate effectively. The fact is that people often hear what they want to hear. Knowing this, you can keep trying until you receive the proper feedback. The negative aspect of this is that it can cause the other person to become defensive, which also will hinder the communication process. Problems in perception can be caused by dissimilar attitudes, different cultural backgrounds, different educational or professional backgrounds, difficulties with the language used, and so on. If you are aware that such conditions exist, you can attempt to minimize the problems that they might cause.

Imagery

This area of communication currently is receiving much attention. If one can use speech to create an image in the learners' heads, and that if that image facilitates learning, then one has learned to use an excellent tool. Analogies and verbal illustrations can help to create imagery. For instance, the learners may be requested to think of (picture) a ferris wheel before the trainer begins to explain how a water wheel works.

EXERCISES

1. When you are trying to explain to someone how to do something, it often seems that the harder you try, the more difficult it becomes. To illustrate this, find someone who is willing to be a learner. Have that person sit down with a pencil and a blank piece of paper. The learner's task is to draw the picture shown in Figure 10, according to the verbal instructions provided by you. Your task is to explain to the learner how to draw the picture. As you may have guessed, there is a catch. You may not rehearse; you may not show the picture; you may use no visual aids; and you must *keep your hands at your sides!* The object is for the learner to draw the picture exactly as it appears in Figure 10. When you are through, discuss the experience with the other person. What restrictions made the task most difficult?

2. Hearing yourself talk on a recording or seeing yourself on television is a peculiar sensation, and it can be very beneficial to a trainer. For this exercise, make a tape recording of your voice, preferably while you are giving one of your training presentations. If videotape also is available, by all means use it. As you listen to the replay, pay attention to your intonation, volume, slurs, ers and ahs, and degree of enthusiasm and believability (i.e., do you sound like someone who knows and cares about the subject?). If you have used videotape, watch your gestures and body language. Do they help or hinder your communication?

3. Find a written paragraph on any subject of interest to you and turn it into an oral presentation. A very formal piece using academic terms would be well suited for this. Your objective is to reword the paragraph, using simple language, so that it can be spoken. Add illustrations that you have developed.

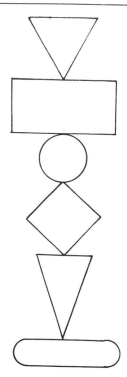

Figure 10. A One-Way Communication Exercise

NONVERBAL COMMUNICATION

People also communicate with gestures, facial expressions, and their bodies. The trainer must be aware of mannerisms and other physical behavior because of their impact on the communication process. For example, you can tell a person that something is all right, but if you shake your fist and glare while doing so, the person will receive precisely the opposite message.

It has been said that everything we do is communication. Culture is communication. The cultural background of people has a strong influence on their communication processes, and this includes nonverbal as well as verbal communication.

Body Language

Social scientists are still learning about how we communicate with our bodies. Even so, much has been determined about this popular and interesting concept. For example, people can communicate interest, enthusiasm, boredom, or withdrawal merely by the ways in which they are sitting. Awareness of body language can help trainers to be better communicators. A few selected references on the subject are included at the end of this chapter.

Some Guidelines

Body language is important to instructional settings. Some positive gestures and positions are:
- open posture
- arms outspread
- body learning forward
- hands at side
- open palms
- relaxed appearance

Some negative postures (notice how important the hands are):
- arms crossed
- hands in pockets
- hands clasped or clenched
- chin in hand
- hands hidden
- legs tightly crossed
- tense appearance

Some examples of body language in training settings are shown in Table 2.

Table 2. Examples of Body Language in Training Settings

In appropriate circumstances, trainees and trainers may be expressing:	When they:
1. Willingness to listen	rub their hands together; lean their heads or bodies forward; rest their chins on the palms of their hands.
2. Friendly feelings	smile frequently; unbutton their jackets or shirts; maintain good eye contact; keep their hands and fingers still; uncross their legs or arms.
3. Approval	pat someone's hair; touch someone's shoulder.
4. Deep thought	pinch the bridges of their noses.
5. Desire to interrupt	tug their ears; raise their index fingers to their lips; flick their hands upward a few inches; place their hands on the speaker's arm.
6. Frustration	give a karate-like chop to their other hands; pound their clenched fists on the table or their palms.
7. Disapproval or rejection	rub or touch their noses with one of their fingers; button their jackets or shirts.
8. Defensive feelings	cross their arms across their chests; cross their legs.

Table 2 (continued)

9. Superiority	steeple their fingers; hold their coat lapels; point to another person with their fingers; cross their legs over the arms of their chairs.
10. Procrastination	idly mouth their pencils or pens; clean their eyeglasses.
11. Stay away, don't bother me	place their hands on their brows; lower their heads; place their feet on their desks or tables.
12. Interaction is finished	shift their postures so that they are no longer facing the people they are talking to; raise their heads; stand up with their papers or personal belongings.

From *Instructional Technique* by Ivor K. Davies. Copyright © 1981 by McGraw-Hill, Inc. Used with permission of McGraw-Hill Book Company.

Distance

Another consideration in nonverbal communication is distance. The distance that people generally maintain when communicating has been determined as follows:[4]

Intimate Distance

- close phase: close physical contact
- far phase: six to eighteen inches (not considered proper in public by Americans)

---

[4]Excerpts from *The Hidden Dimension* by Edward T. Hall. Copyright © 1966 by Edward T. Hall. Reprinted by permission of Doubleday & Company, Inc., and Blassingame, McCauley & Wood.

Personal Distance

- close phase (one and one-half to two and one-half feet): comfortable if the people know one another
- far phase (two and one-half to four feet): arm's length

Social Distance

- close phase (four to seven feet): impersonal business
- far phase (seven to twelve feet): more formal communication

Public Distance

- close phase (twelve to twenty-five feet): can get away
- far phase (twenty-five feet or more): set around important public figures.

As can be seen, the distance that is accepted is based on the relationship between the people involved and the circumstances. Depending on the physical nature of the learning environment, the type of training, and the trainer's and learners' personalities and perceptions, the training process would be categorized somewhere within the personal and social distance scales.

SUMMARY

How well the trainer communicates with the learners will play a major role in the ultimate success of a training event. The elements of the communication process are: sender, receiver, message, and channel. Feedback that the message was received and understood closes the communication loop. Anything less is not complete communication. Some other key points are:

- Simplicity is essential.

● Mere words are the least effective means of communicating.
● Body language is communication, whether it is
intended to be so or not.

SELECTED REFERENCES

Communications Research Associates. *Communicate: A workbook for interpersonal communication* (2nd ed.). Dubuque,
IA: Kendall/Hunt, 1978.

Farb, P. *Word play: What happens when people talk.* New York:
Bantam, 1973.

Fast, J. *Body language.* New York: Pocket Books, 1970.

Flesch, R. *The art of plain talk.* New York: Harper & Row, 1946.
(All of Flesch's works on communication are excellent.)

Hall, E.T. *The silent language.* New York: Anchor, 1959.

Luthi, J.R. Communicating Communication. In J.W. Pfeiffer & J.E.
Jones (Eds.), *The 1978 annual handbook for group facilitators.*
San Diego, CA: University Associates, 1978.

Nierenberg, G.I., & Calero, H.H. *How to read a person like a book.*
New York: Pocket Books, 1971.

Shannon, W.C. One-person communication. *Training and Development Journal,* May, 1978, 20-24.

ANSWERS TO EXERCISE ON PAGES 94 and 95

1. Any employee found to be intoxicated on the job will
be suspended immediately. An investigation and report will
be made within two days by the employee's supervisor.

2. Employees who work thirty hours or more per week
will work *only* during the hours prescribed for their depart-
ments.

Chapter 8
Active Listening

Active listening is not merely a tool to use in interviewing or in helping situations, it is a technique that is applicable to and useful in everyday life.

When you have completed this chapter, you will be able to:

- identify the steps in the active listening process,
- use active listening in the training setting,
- identify the other forms of communication response that are less desirable.

ACTIVE VERSUS PASSIVE LISTENING

A trainer must be an astute learner. Understanding what the learners are saying can make a great deal of difference in how much learning takes place. Learners have plenty to say, and the trainer can learn a lot from them—about their learning needs, about their reactions to the training, about the content, and so forth.

One way to listen is to quietly absorb the statements and questions of the other person. This is called passive listening. It is used effectively in therapeutic situations in which the speaker merely may need to have someone to talk to. This type of listening can be enhanced by throwing in an occasional, passive response such as "Uh hmm," "Oh?," or "I see." You may, at some time, be in the role of therapist to a learner, but it is hoped that this will not occur often.

The problem with more passive forms of listening is that they are passive. The best learning environment is an active, stimulating one, in which things are happening. Simply stated, active listening is the process of getting the sender of a message (learner) *involved* with the receiver (trainer). One of the main results of this process is two-way communication. Active listening, when it causes two-way communication, yields two conditions that all training strives for:

- *getting the learner involved* in the learning process,
- *facilitating* the art and science of *problem solving*.

Active listening can create effective discussions of specific subject matter and can aid in recognizing problems and determining who is to solve them. The technique of active listening is a key feature of Thomas Gordon's parent, teacher, and leadership effectiveness training (**PET, TET, LET**).

HOW ACTIVE LISTENING WORKS

The steps in active listening are:
1. The sender sends a coded message.
2. The receiver receives the message.
3. The receiver decodes the message.
4. The receiver feeds back *what the message is—nothing more or less—with no evaluations.*
5. The sender (now a receiver, too) either agrees with the receiver's interpretation or, if not, starts the message over again.

Stated more briefly, the receiver tunes into what the other person is saying, feeding back the receiver's understanding at appropriate points. For example:

Learner: Why does step "C" have to be completed before going to step "D"?

Trainer: It is not clear to you why the steps in the process we are studying have to be done in the order given?

Learner: Right. It seems to me that it would not hurt to change the order around.

The receiver now knows what the problem is. Either the receiver has failed to make it clear why a precise order is required or else the learner has not been paying attention. Just to answer the question at hand may be insufficient; the learner may be having difficulty understanding the whole process. Active listening can help to discover this.

Sometimes a question disguises some other problem or feeling. Active listening can help to determine this. For example:

Learner: What you just said does not make sense.

Trainer: What I just said about this new concept does not make sense to you, does it?

Learner: No. I was doing fine until now, but none of this new stuff seems to sink in.

In this case, the feedback to the sender confirms that the real problem is that the sender (learner) is having difficulty with the new subject matter, not just with the latest statement made by the trainer. Note that the trainer did not include any evaluation in the feedback. The purpose of active listening is to clarify the message, not to offer your response to it.

THE BENEFITS OF USING ACTIVE LISTENING

A number of good things can happen if you use active listening appropriately.

- It shows the learners (or whoever is communicating to you) that you want to hear what they have to say.
- It relieves you of the position of having all the answers and acknowledges that learners have something to say, too.
- It allows you to get closer to the learners through open, honest communication.
- It recognizes the feeling part of communication between people. If negative feelings exist, they can be brought out and dealt with.
- It helps to overcome resistance on the part of the learners.

- It improves the chances for people who are silent and/or dependent to become involved in the learning process.
- It keeps the problem where it belongs—with the learner—and provides a forum for it to be resolved immediately.
- It encourages the sender to keep communication going, because it does not evaluate or steer the communication away from the sender's original intent.

SOME THINGS TO AVOID

According to Gordon,[5] there are a dozen ways to respond to people who are communicating with us. Successful active listening includes avoiding these types of responses:

- ordering, directing, commanding
- warning, admonishing, threatening
- exhorting, moralizing, preaching
- advising, giving solutions or suggestions
- lecturing, teaching, giving logical arguments
- judging, criticizing, disagreeing, blaming
- praising, agreeing
- name calling, ridiculing, shaming
- interpreting, analyzing, diagnosing
- reassuring, sympathizing, consoling, supporting
- probing, questioning, interrogating
- withdrawing, distracting, humoring, diverting

There certainly are times when several of these categories of response also can be successful. For instance, questioning is an excellent instructional tool (see Chapter 11 for more on this). However, it would not be appropriate in a situation in which active listening is appropriate.

---

[5]Reprinted with permission from the book *PET: Parent Effectiveness Training* by Dr. Thomas Gordon. Copyright © 1970. Published by David McKay Company, Inc.

Questioning, or any of the other responses mentioned previously, may cause the sender to feel that the message is not accepted as is. In some situations, the sender will then become defensive, "clam up," or attempt to change the message so that it is acceptable to the receiver. By using active listening, the receiver tries to step into the shoes of the sender—to empathize. This can help the sender to clarify the message, and is a powerful tool in problem solving or in other helping situations.

TO PUT IT ALL TOGETHER

Active listening is a tool to get the right answers, or feelings, from learners. It is a natural way to help someone to communicate. It opens the door to a two-way interpersonal communication and keeps it open.

Active listening does not imply that you agree with what the sender said. It merely means that you have heard the message that was intended. You do not accept the problems or values of the sender, but you can use active listening to help the sender to resolve them. Of course, you do not have to wait until a learner has a problem to use active listening; it can be a valuable tool in other situations as well.

EXERCISES

1. Putting yourself in the role of trainer (receiver), write down a response that you feel illustrates the concept of active listening for each of the following statements or questions.

   a. *Learner:* How can anyone ever remember all nine of those rules you just gave us?

   Receiver:

   b. *Learner:* When are we going to stop all this lecture business and get our hands on the machine?

   Receiver:

c. *Learner:* Can't you give me a better example of what you are talking about . . . something out of real life?

Receiver:

d. *Learner:* I thought we were supposed to have a coffee break by now.

Receiver:

e. *Learner:* I stayed up until midnight reading the assignment, and I sure don't remember reading that.

Receiver:

2. Use active listening at every appropriate opportunity for the next few weeks. This includes work, home (especially if you have children), and all your interpersonal relationships. Note how often you discover that there was a lot of difference between what was said and the true message.

3. Refer to the twelve forms of response on page 108 and note those that you use most often in your everyday communications. What responses do you typically use in various situations? Do you see any pattern to this? Could you use a more appropriate response in any of these situations?

SUMMARY

Showing empathy to others is essential to being successful in a helping field such as training. Active listening is one way to show empathy. It is a way to inform the sender of a message that the receiver is open to the message. In active listening, the receiver attempts to feed back the full content of the message to the sender, without adding any evaluation, instruction, direction, and so on. Active listening is a useful technique in determining hidden messages and in problem solving.

SELECTED REFERENCES

As already noted, Gordon's works feature the technique of active listening. All his books contain excellent material on this topic.

Communications Research Associates. *Communicate: A workbook for interpersonal communication.* Dubuque, IA: Kendall/ Hunt, 1978.

Gordon, T. *Leader effectiveness training.* New York: Wyden Books, 1977.

Gordon, T. *P.E.T.: Parent effectiveness training.* New York: New American Library, 1975.

Gordon, T. *Teacher effectiveness training.* New York: David McKay, 1974.

Wismer, J.N. Communication effectiveness: Active listening and sending feeling messages. In J.W. Pfeiffer and J.E. Jones (Eds.), *The 1978 annual handbook for group facilitators.* San Diego, CA: University Associates, 1978.

ANSWERS TO EXERCISE ON PAGES 109 AND 110

The following are *possible* receiver responses to the examples given:

a. You don't see how anyone can remember so much? *or:* You don't understand why there are so many rules to remember?

b. You're anxious to get your hands on the machine? *or:* You're ready to stop the lecture and get on to the practical work?

c. The example isn't realistic to you? *or:* You feel that a more realistic example would be better.

d. You expected to take a break by now? *or:* You're ready to take a break now?

e. You worked for a long time getting ready for this lesson. *or:* You don't believe that the point just covered was in the reading assignment?

Chapter 9
Transactional Analysis As
a Communication Tool

Transactional anaylsis (TA) provides a means for improving interpersonal communications.

When you have completed this chapter, you will be able to:

- state the three basic scripts by which people live,
- identify which scripts others are using,
- apply the knowledge and techniques of TA to your role as a trainer.

WHAT IS TA?

If you go to your favorite book store and take a look at the section featuring self-help books or at the family or education sections, you will find a lot of books about transactional analysis. This provides a clue to how well-received and useful the process is. You also may have heard some of the TA jargon: scripts, games, tapes, being O.K., not O.K., win/win, win/lose.

Transactional analysis is a tool that can help you to improve your interpersonal relations—how well you perceive, communicate with, and assist others. It is a method of analysis by which one person can determine the basis from which another individual is communicating or interacting and, thus, decide how best to respond. It is a tool that can be used in all life situations, as well as in the training setting.

113

Anything you can do that will help you to understand better where others are "coming from," what their true feelings are, and what they are trying to say certainly will contribute to your success as a trainer.

THREE DIFFERENT PEOPLE IN ONE

According to TA theory, there are really three aspects or roles in each of us: the parent, the adult, and the child. The way in which we communicate or react to stimuli identifies the role in which we currently are operating. No one operates constantly from the same role. According to TA theory, it is all right to assume any one of the three roles if the circumstances warrant it. Generally, however, it is most efficient and desirable to function in the adult role.

A Tape Recorder in Your Head

People function from the point of view of parent, adult, and child—and fluctuate in these roles—because of scripts that have been etched into their brains—the tape recorders of their minds. Because individual learning and early training vary, people's scripts (or ways of operating) vary.

To illustrate, let us imagine that a stranger is seen walking dangerously close to a hot fire pit. Here are three messages that the onlooker might send, one from each mode:

Parent: "Get away from that fire!"

Adult: "There is another path here that is much safer than the one you are on."

Child: "You sure must like to get burned."

In most cases, the adult would create the most positive basis for communication by treating the receiver on an adult, equal basis. If, however, the stranger were about to be seriously burned, the appropriate mode probably would be to turn on the parent tape. There are times, too, when the child tape has its place, for example, when humor is needed.

Here is an example that is related to the trainer's role:

Parent: "You are going to learn this skill if it is the last thing I do."

Adult: "You have mastered all the skills up to this point, so I'm sure that, with a little effort, you will master this one, too."

Child: "You sure can't do that very well, can you?"

In some cases, it seems as though people are programmed to react (communicate) in certain ways. To a large extent, this is true. If you are a parent, you automatically respond just as your parents did. The adult mode sometimes is difficult to achieve, let alone to sustain.

The PAC Circle

Communications are two-way transactions. This is where the analysis part of TA becomes very useful. If a person speaking in the adult mode is responded to as an adult, the communication is likely to be successful. If the respondent also is speaking from the adult mode, so much the better. Problems arise when someone who is speaking as an adult is responded to as a parent or a child. This is called a crossed transaction, and is illustrated in Figure 11.

An example of the first uncrossed (adult-adult) transaction is as follows:

Trainer: There will be a test tomorrow. (adult)

Learner: Good, I'm ready for it. (adult)

The second uncrossed transaction might go like this:

Trainer: You looked puzzled. Shall I explain that last point one more time? (adult to adult)

Learner: Wow, thanks. Maybe I will get it this time. (child to adult)

An uncrossed transaction, in TA terms, is "O.K."

The crossed transactions, the ones that do not achieve successful, closed-loop communication, are illustrated in the lower portion of the figure. The first example might happen as follows:

Trainer: There will be a test tomorrow. (adult)

Learner: We just had one and, besides, I'm not ready. (child to parent)

The second crossed transaction can be illustrated as follows:

Trainer: You look puzzled. Shall I explain that last point one more time? (adult)

Learner: If you were a decent trainer, you would not have to keep going over everything twice. (parent to child)

These crossed transactions are "not O.K."

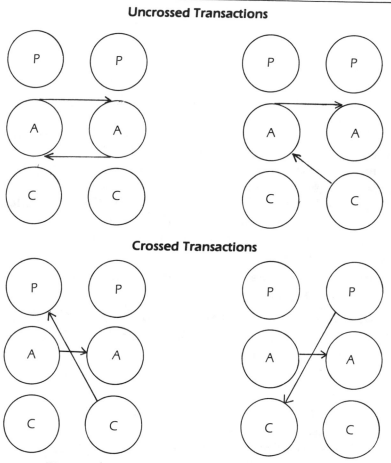

Figure 11. Analyses of Possible Transactions

The matrix in Table 3 provides a capsule of the PAC concept.

Table 3. Cues for Determining PAC Communication State

	Parent Ego State	Adult Ego State	Child Ego State
Vocal Tone	Condescending, putting down, criticizing, or accusing	Matter-of-fact	Full of feeling
Words Used	Everyone knows that . . . You should never . . .	How, what, when, why, who, probable	I'm mad at you! Hey, great (or any words that have a high feeling level)
Posture	Puffed up, overly correct, very proper	Attentive, eye-to-eye, listening and looking for maximum data	Slouching, playful, beat down or burdened, self-conscious
Facial Expression	Frowning, worried or disapproving, chin jutting out	Alert eyes, paying close attention	Excitement, surprise, downcast eyes, quivering lips or chin, moist eyes
Bodily Gestures	Hands on hips, finger pointing in accusation, arms folded across chest	Leaning forward in chair toward other person, moving closer to hear and see better	Spontaneous activity, wringing of hands, pacing, withdrawing into corner or moving away from other, laughter, raising hand for permission

From "PAC at Work" by Lyman K. Randall. In Communications Research Associates, *Communicate* (2nd ed.). Dubuque, IA: Kendall/ Hunt, 1978. Reprinted by permission of the author.

You can see at a glance that the trainer should operate from the adult role (called the adult ego state in the matrix).

EXERCISES

1. The following are several statements or questions made from the viewpoint of a trainer, each followed by a possible learner reply. Referring to the four types of transactions in Figure 11, determine which type each of the following transactions is. Remember: A◄─►A; A─►A and A◄─C are O.K.; A─►A and C◄─P; A─►A and P◄─C are crossed transactions and are not O.K.

   a. *Sender:* Did you have any trouble with the exercise?
      Respondent: Yes, but with a little extra effort, I got it done.

   b. *Sender:* I know that mastering this performance objective is tough, but it is pivotal to the rest of the workshop.
      Respondent: Okay, I'll keep trying, even if it kills us both.

   c. *Sender:* When several of you come in late, it is not fair to the others to repeat material.
      Respondent: What's the matter, don't you like me?

   d. *Sender:* When several of you come in late, it is not fair to the others to repeat material.
      Respondent: You are right. I think we should all strive to be on time from now on.

   e. *Sender:* Did you have any trouble with the exercise?
      Respondent: Of course I did. You know better than to give such a hard problem.

   f. *Sender:* I know that mastering this performance objective is tough, but it is pivotal to the rest of the workshop.
      Respondent: Then why don't you do a better job of preparing us?

2. Observe your own (as well as other) communication exchanges for several days. See how difficult or easy it is to spot a wide variety of crossed situations. Conversely, observe how often you see an adult-to-adult exchange.

POSITIVE STROKES AND WARM FUZZIES

Many people like to collect things. Almost everyone likes to collect "strokes"—verbal caresses or compliments. In TA terminology, this is referred to as "stamp collecting." Individual life scripts determine how important strokes are and what kind of strokes are required.

Throughout most of this book, and especially in Chapter 3, it is stressed that trainers should provide positive feedback, or strokes. These also have been called "warm fuzzies," e.g., "You did a great job of answering that question"; "It has been a pleasure to be with you people today"; or "Keep up the good work."

People need strokes. One of your roles as a trainer is to distribute warm fuzzies each day during the training session. It is a habit that will enhance learning.

PLAYING GAMES

Unfortunately, some people collect negative strokes, the so-called "cold pricklies." Transactional analysis refers to this, the culmination of a not-O.K. life script and crossed transactions, as "playing games." Perhaps we all, on occasion, find ourselves playing some of the games that are categorized and named in the TA literature. "Victim" is one game, and it is pretty self-explanatory.

Some games are designed to attain specific results such as proving a point. Others are designed to never achieve a closed-loop status, such as a child offering excuse after excuse about why its toys cannot be picked up and put away. The purpose of such a game is to provide a payoff—usually a negative one—for the person who is playing it. The payoff may be anger, rejection, or simply attention.

As a trainer, rather than a therapist, you will not need to know a great deal about TA games, but several of the references at the end of this chapter will provide you with more information if you desire it. For training purposes, it is sufficient to communicate on an adult basis and let it be known that you expect the other person to do likewise. In this way, you can avoid playing games and will have more effective communication as well.

SUMMARY

Transactional analysis (TA) offers an excellent means of understanding and improving relationships between people and can be useful to trainers as a tool in communicating. Some key points regarding TA are:

- People live according to learned life scripts; they operate from either a parent, adult, or child mode.
- The adult mode is the most effective, although the other modes can be O.K. at times.
- Adult-adult communication is the best in most situations.
- People like to receive positive strokes. Fair distribution of them can enhance the trainer's role.

SELECTED REFERENCES

Much has been written about transactional analysis, and it has been applied to a multitude of situations, professions, and solutions. The following represents a broad range of references, from the short and simple to the more complex.

Anderson, J.P. A transactional analysis primer. In J.E. Jones & J.W. Pfeiffer (Eds.), *The 1973 annual handbook for group facilitators*. San Diego, CA: University Associates, 1973.

Berne, E. *Games people play*. New York: Grove Press, 1964.

Berne, E. *What do you say after you say hello*. New York: Bantam, 1972.

Bradford, J.A., & Guberman, R. *Transactional awareness*. Reading, MA: Addison-Wesley, 1978.

Communications Research Associates. *Communicate: A workbook for interpersonal communication* (2nd ed.). Dubuque, IA: Kendall/Hunt, 1978.

Harris, T.A. *I'm OK—you're OK*. New York: Avon, 1967.

James, M., & Jongeward, D. *Born to win*. Reading, MA: Addison-Wesley, 1971.

James, M. *The OK boss*. Reading, MA: Addison-Wesley, 1975.

Jongward, D., & James, M. *Winning with people*. Reading, MA: Addison-Wesley, 1973.

Meininger, J. *Success through transactional analysis*. New York: Grosset and Dunlap, 1973.

ANSWERS TO EXERCISE 1 ON PAGE 118

All initial statements/questions are adult to adult. The replies are:

    a. adult to adult (O.K.)

    b. child to adult (O.K.)

    c. child to parent (not O.K., crossed)

    d. adult to adult (O.K.)

    e. parent to child (not O.K., crossed)

    f. parent to child (not O.K., crossed)

Chapter 10
Motivating Learners

Getting and keeping learners excited about the learning process is a challenge. Doing so makes the process more productive and enjoyable for everyone.

When you have completed this chapter, you will be able to:

- state several key points about what motivates people,
- state who is responsible for what in the process of motivation,
- exercise some influence on motivation in a learning environment by using the principles that you have learned.

When the subject of motivation is discussed, many people think of Dale Carnegie (*How to Win Friends and Influence People*), Norman Vincent Peale (*The Power of Positive Thinking*), Napoleon Hill (*Think and Grow Rich*), or any of countless other "experts." The concept of motivation also is commonly linked with the training provided for salespersons. Yet motivation plays an important part in the learning process. Lack of it can seriously inhibit how much learning takes place.

Obviously, the trainer cannot completely control the motivation of the learners. There are numerous influences in the life of each learner that have an effect on that person's level of motivation. In addition, the source of motivation is somewhat nebulous; what turns one person on may do just the opposite to another. However, because motivation is so important in learning, knowledge of how you may (or may not) be able to influence it is a necessary training tool.

PSYCHOLOGICAL MOTIVES

From basic psychology, we know that there are two classes of motives that determine our behavior: physiological motives (e.g., hunger, thirst, sexual drives, cold) and psychological motives (e.g., cognitive, achievement). The physiological motives are, obviously, quite basic. The psychological ones are learned. The cognitive motives, which also may be basic, include the human attributes of curiosity and the seeking of challenge. These are part of the natural tendency of people to need to feel competent and self-determined.

The following are some interesting facets of motivation behavior:

- Behavior caused by motivation is instigated by the need for something (to make up a deficit) or to gain something (incentive).
- Human beings are goal oriented.
- Motivation behavior is directed *toward* something.
- It is selective (i.e., the person chooses the behavior that is most apt to satisfy the motive).
- It can be satisfied.
- Some behaviors are not related to any type of motivation.
- The offer of a reward does not always serve as a motivation.

Trainers do need to pay some attention to physiological motives. Three hours between coffee breaks might have a decided negative effect on learning. Furthermore, there certainly should be concern for the cognitive motives. The fact that people are naturally curious and seek to establish goals has a positive effect on the learning process. The achievement motive, however, is of most interest to trainers. Most people need to achieve. One element in this may be fear of failure. Some people are more strongly influenced by this than others. The higher a person's need to achieve, the easier it is to motivate the person. (The exceptions are the few people who are "driven" to achieve and those who actually fear success.)

Another motive that can enhance the learning setting is that people need to be with other people. Of course, there are loners; and we all like to have some solitude at times; yet, people are attracted to groups.

The power motive also may have an effect on learning, because knowledge and skill can lead to greater capability, which can be converted to power. The power motive drives many people, to one extent or another.

THEORIES OF MOTIVATION

Many theories regarding motivation have been researched and documented. Some are useful in gaining an under-standing of the importance of motivation to training. Four of these—McGregor's Theory X and Theory Y; Maslow's hierarchy of needs; Herzberg's motivation-hygiene theory; and adult learning theory—are presented here. Knowledge of these theories can aid the trainer in relating to learners and in using positive motivational techniques.

McGregor's Theory X and Theory Y

McGregor was a proponent of a participative approach to management, as opposed to a more autocratic style.[6] Theory X is the label given to the traditional, more authoritarian approach, and Theory Y refers to the more humanistic, participative style. The Theory X view holds that people inherently dislike work and will avoid it if at all possible and, because of this, extreme measures and strong control are required to accomplish work. Part of this theory is that, because of lack of ambition and need for security, people want to be directed. Conversely, Theory Y states that hard work is natural and that people will take it on themselves to achieve goals and objectives. Theory Y says that people like rewards, are imaginative and creative, and will seek responsibility.

---

[6]Douglas McGregor, *The Human Side of Enterprise.* New York: McGraw-Hill, 1960.

Both approaches work, whether used by an executive, parent, trainer, or anyone in a position of authority. There are times when Theory X is preferred, such as in the commonly cited example of the military commander in the heat of battle. In most situations, however, one is apt to discover styles that are somewhere in between. From a trainer's perspective, the motivational approach inherent in Theory Y—the more participative approach—is much better suited to adult learning.

Maslow's Hierarchy of Needs

Maslow's hierarchy is one of the most commonly referenced works in the study of motivation. His theory is that a person's needs (shown in Table 4) are met in order, starting with the most basic—physiological needs—and moving up to self-actualization. Not everyone is believed to achieve total self-fulfillment, but those who do are considered to be the most psychologically healthy people. As a trainer, it might be helpful to think of learners as attempting to move toward the esteem and self-actualization needs as their motivation for being in the learning environment.

Herzberg's Motivation-Hygiene Theory

The work done by Herzberg resulted in two categories of factors that motivate people: motivator factors and hygiene (maintenance) factors.[7] The motivator factors are achievement, recognition of achievement, work itself, responsibility, advancement, and the possibility of growth. The hygiene factors are supervision, company policy and administration, working conditions, relations with others, status, job security, salary, and personal life. Although these factors primarily relate to work, they easily can be equated with the training setting. The theory is that people are motivated to *work* by the motivator factors. The hygiene factors need to

---

[7]Frederick Herzberg, *Work and the Nature of Man*. New York: New American Library, 1966.

be present, but only to *maintain* performance. Herzberg's theory says that hygiene factors do not actually motivate performance and are noticed only if deficient in some way.

Table 4. Maslow's Hierarchy of Needs

Needs (in descending order of importance)	Characteristics
Self-actualization	Realizing full potential; achieving height of one's capacity; achieving desire for self-fulfillment.
Esteem	High self-evaluation; self-respect; desire for strength; achievement, adequacy, mastery, competence, confidence, independence, and freedom; prestige, recognitiion, and appreciation.
Belongingness and love	Desire for affection, relationships with others, becoming part of a group; being accepted by others.
Safety	Security, stability; dependency, protection; freedom from fear, anxiety, and chaos; need for law and order, structure.
Physiological	Satisfaction of hunger and thirst, and need for sex and air.
Other Needs	
Cognitive	To know and understand; to satisfy curiosity.
Aesthetic	Beauty, order, symmetry, structure in surroundings.

Data based on Hierarchy of Needs in "A Theory of Human Motivation": In *Motivation and Personality* (2nd ed.) by Abraham H. Maslow. Copyright © 1970 by Abraham H. Maslow. Reprinted by permission of Harper & Row Publishers, Inc.

Adult Learning Theory

An overview of adult learning theory was presented in Chapter 3. A review of this will reveal a close correlation between some of those principles and the concepts just discussed. For instance, there is a great deal of similarity between the idea of self-directed learning in adults and

Theory Y, esteem needs, and motivator factors. In addition to self-direction, some adult learning principles are:

- Adults are motivated to learn when they perceive the need for their learning.
- Adults relate the subject matter to their own life experiences.
- Adult learning is most effective when it is oriented to the real world.
- Adult learning should vary depending on the individual differences among the learners.

There is no one theory that explains what makes people tick and, more specifically, what motivates them to learn. Culture has something to do with it, as do Maslow's needs hierarchy, Herzberg's theory, and so on. The probability is that *several* motives are responsible for the behavior of learners. Awareness of this fact and knowledge of the related theories can help the trainer to make the learning experience easier and more successful.

WHO IS RESPONSIBLE FOR WHAT

There are three inputs to the motivational process as far as training is concerned: the trainer, the learner, and outside forces. This is shown in Figure 12. Outside forces are people—family, friends, employer, associates—and events in the learner's life. Of the three, the trainer can control one: the trainer's input. The trainer may or may not be able to exert any influence on the input of the learner, but cannot control it at all. The trainer usually can do nothing about the outside influences.

The trainer's obligation is to do the best he or she can and to try to influence the learner to make a positive input. If the learner has just been kicked out of the house by a spouse or told by a boss that the training had better end soon so that some work can get done, there is little that the trainer alone can do.

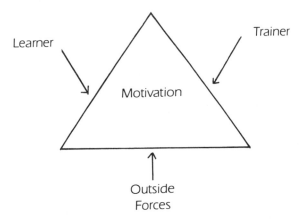

Figure 12. The Process of Motivation

WHAT MORE CAN BE DONE

Even if you give little thought to motivation as a training technique but strive to implement the concepts of sound training technology (e.g., being prepared, making your presentations relevant and interesting), motivation will be influenced positively. In other words, good training has built-in motivation. If you add to this a conscious effort to encourage the learner's own motivations, based on the theories presented in this chapter, you will be ahead of the game. In addition, there are a few other things that you can do to help motivate learners:

- Set a good personal example. Be well-prepared and professional in your manner; make it obvious that you work hard at what you do and are happy and satisfied in doing it.
- Have a positive attitude. Let the learners know that you care.
- Present models, such as successful people who have benefited from the same training that the current learners are undergoing.
- Provide rewards where appropriate.

- Provide positive challenges.
- Treat the learners as adults.
- Never degrade anyone.

EXERCISE

The people-oriented approach to motivation is the one that is advocated for training facilitators. Next to each of the motivational factors listed below, list *at least* one thing that you might do to implement and otherwise take advantage of the factor in your role as a trainer. Some possible actions are listed at the end of this chapter.

1. achievement

2. responsibility

3. reward

4. recognition

5. advancement

6. self-directedness

SUMMARY

The concept of motivation can be applied (on a positive basis) to enhance the learning situation. People can be motivated to perform, and learn, better. Some of the key points from this chapter are:

- People basically are achievers; they seek goals.
- Higher goals, such as achievement, success, recognition, and rewards, are more apt to motivate the

learning process than lesser needs such as security and salary.

● Motivation is influenced by the trainer, the learner, and outside factors. The trainer can control but one of these three influences.

● From the point of view of training, motivation theory and adult learning principles are closely related.

SELECTED REFERENCES

Virtually any good, introductory, psychology text will provide background on the basics of motivation. Other pertinent references are:

Harrison, R. A practical model of motivation and character development. In J.E. Jones & J.W. Pfeiffer (Eds.), *The 1979 annual handbook for group facilitators.* San Diego, CA: University Associates, 1979.

Herzberg, F. *Work and the nature of man.* New York: New American Library, 1966.

Knowles, M. *The adult learner: A neglected species* (2nd ed.). Houston: Gulf, 1978.

Mager, R.F. *Developing attitude toward learning.* Belmont, CA: Fearon-Pitman, 1968.

Maslow, A.H. *Motivation and personality* (2nd ed.). New York: Harper & Row, 1970.

McGregor, D. *The human side of enterprise.* New York: McGraw-Hill, 1960.

ANSWERS TO EXERCISE ON PAGE 130

1. Point out that on completion of the event, the learner will join the relatively small group of people who are now qualified to perform in the role (for which the training was designed).

2. Develop self-paced, individualized materials.

3. Provide certificates of completion.

4. Praise high achievers as soon as they have demonstrated satisfactory performance. (For that matter, praise

anyone who has demonstrated satisfactory performance and encourage those who have not.)

5. Relate the learning to its place as a stepping stone for job advancement.

6. Have the learners develop their own check lists for completion of the training. (The sample answer for number 2 above also could apply here.)

Chapter 11
Getting People Involved

The name of the game in training is to get the learners involved. The quantity and quality of learning that takes place is directly proportional to the degree of learner involvement.

When you have completed this chapter, you will be able to:

- state the importance of getting learners involved in training,
- identify several methods of doing so,
- use one or more of the methods, including the technique of questioning.

People learn by doing. The growing trend in training over the years has been to get the learners more involved. One way to do this—a way that has gained in popularity—is to give the learner most of, if not all, the responsibility for learning. Some of the words related to this are self-paced, individualized, computer-assisted, learner-controlled, and programmed instruction. The home-study market is enormous and is growing at a tremendous rate. Relatively inexpensive microprocessors have spurred the computerization of training to new levels. But, barring total automation of all training, trainers will be needed to design training and to get it automated. The trainer's function is, and will continue to be, to facilitate the learning process by getting the learners as involved in the process as possible.

The previous chapters of this book have presented several excellent techniques for promoting learner involvement. The best methods to achieve learner involvement are those that you have adapted to fit your own situation and with which you feel comfortable. However, there are a number of techniques designed specifically for this important aspect of training. One of the most tried and true of these techniques is to ask questions.

ASK QUESTIONS

Asking questions can help you to be more effective as a trainer. The technique has been used with success by trainers and educators for thousands of years. If you think back to your own learning experiences, the chances are that the instructors and teachers who most influenced your learning were the ones who challenged you—with questions in one form or another.

Questions serve a variety of purposes in a variety of instructional situations.

They arouse interest. People are naturally curious. Questions can help to get them "hooked" on the subject matter.

They stimulate thinking. People's minds need to be kept busy while learning is taking place. One way to cause that to happen is to ask questions. When the learners start to ask their own questions, it is a sign that the "pumps have been primed."

They keep people on track. The importance of achieving learning objectives already has been mentioned. Questions directed toward the objectives of the session help to ensure that those objectives are achieved. There will be days when it will take everything you have to keep the minds of your group members from wandering. Asking the right questions can help to put you back where you want to be.

They solicit information. The ultimate test to determine if learning has been effective is a demonstration of how well the skill and/or knowledge is applied afterwards. Tests given at various stages during the instructional process can give good clues about what has and has not been learned, but the best time to find that out is at the time that the learning takes place. Responses to questions provide indications of how well the learners understand the material.

They get learners involved. There is no faster way to get a learner's attention than to fire off a question, especially if it is directed to a specific individual. Answering a question is one way in which a shy person can participate.

Types of Questions

Questions can be classified in at least two ways. It is necessary to understand both types in order to become adept at questioning. The two are open/closed and direct/indirect questions.

Open/Closed Questions

Usually, you would not want to ask many closed questions, the ones that can be answered with a simple answer. The following are examples of closed questions:

- Can anyone tell me who has ultimate leadership authority in a training session? (The actual answer to this question is probably "yes," which means that the question was not phrased properly to begin with. Even if the question begins with "who," it still is a closed—and easy—question. It will not stimulate thinking or discussion.)
- What are three learning principles that an instructor should bear in mind? (There are several possible answers, but any correct combination will finish the interaction, making it a closed question.)

Open questions are the ones that will do the most good. They arouse interest; stimulate thinking; keep the lesson, learners, and instructor on track; provoke feedback; and get the learners involved. Some examples of open questions are:

- Why did you give the answer you did? (This question is useful if the answer given is unusual, if it is correct but it seems that most other participants don't know it, or if it required considerable thought and analysis to arrive at it.)
- What might we do to reinforce the learning of rules?

(This requires the respondent to discuss the principle of practice and transfer of learning and also to show an understanding of why the rules are important.)

- If you saw . . . [a specific situation related to the training], what might you do? (This requires quick thinking and may result in several alternative courses of action.)

Direct/Indirect Questions

The other way to classify questions is according to whom the question is addressed. You can either toss it out to the whole group or you can direct it to a specific individual. Which way is best depends on the situation. Throwing a question first at the group encourages everyone to think about the answer. However, you may find either that people are reluctant to volunteer their answers or that one or two people are answering all the questions. Directing questions to specific individuals helps to even out the distribution and to make sure that everyone (including those who need it most) has a turn.

The rhetorical question, to which no answer is expected, generally is directed at the entire group. This is useful if the question is one that you want to leave for the group members to think about. Rhetorical questions sometimes are used to introduce a subject, but this should be done sparingly, because it can become boring and also can confuse the listeners.

How To Ask Questions

There are a number of tips about asking questions that can help to ensure success.

1. Questions should require *thinking.* Thus, the preference for open-ended questions rather than ones that require only simple answers.
2. It builds confidence in learners if they have a *reasonable chance of answering* the question.

Nothing is gained by asking a question that is virtually impossible to answer (unless you are proving a point).

3. Using questions *in the beginning* of the training session helps you to discover where learners stand and if they are prepared. It also sets the stage for what is about to happen.

4. Using questions *in the middle* of the training session serves as a check on learning and provides a change of pace.

5. Using questions *at the end* of the training helps to summarize and reinforce the learning content and helps you to find out whether or not you have been successful.

6. *Variety* in questioning keeps things more interesting and helps to keep the learners on their toes.

7. Address all questions to *the entire group* first. Then, if a question is to be directed to a particular individual, single out that person. This helps to keep everybody mentally alert.

8. *Distribute questions evenly* so that each person gets a fair number. As a corollary, be careful of appearing to "pick on" certain individuals (even if you feel that they need special attention).

9. *Give positive feedback.* Of course, if an answer is terrible, it is difficult to be positive, but at least do not be negative.

10. *Do not give up too easily or answer the question yourself.* Keep at it. Perhaps you can rephrase the question or break it down into smaller parts.

11. *Keep things simple.* Long, drawn-out questions lead to poor, incomplete answers. Try to keep a question to one main thought.

12. *Do not solicit rote answers.* Closed-ended questions often can be answered with pat, rote answers. In most types of training, however, you will be looking for ideas and understanding, so you will ask open-ended questions. The thought behind the answer is

what you are looking for. Just as in an essay question on a quiz, a variety of answers—some of which are completely original—can be expected.

13. *Who, what, where, when, why, how, and if* are excellent words to use in asking questions.

EXERCISE

Criticize each of the questions that follow and reword it into a question that you feel would be better. (Some possible answers are given at the end of this chapter.)

1. Can you tell me how a person might go about determining the origin of the word barbecue?

2. Why did the California gold rush occur; who were some of the people involved in the process; and what were its economic implications, including considerations of imported foreign labor?

3. Tell me everything you know about audiovisual aids, including whether they are effective.

4. Do you know the difference between a closed question and an open question?

5. How many ways are there to determine whether or not a learner understands a given concept?

WHEN LEARNERS ASK QUESTIONS

Usually, asking questions indicates interest on the part of the learners. You can assume that you must have said or done something to stimulate them, which is what learning is all about. The simplest strategy would seem to be to respond with an answer to the learner's question. This is assuming, of course, that the learner's question is legitimate, and not all of them are. Here are some guidelines to follow in dealing with learner questions; they are followed by a discussion of special circumstances.

1. *Do not answer,* but get someone else to. It is perfectly fair for you to ask someone else to answer a question from the floor.

2. *Solicit comments* on both the question and the potential answers. This is a good way to get a discussion going, and it is the best kind of discussion, because the learners will have generated it.

3. *Do not evade* the question. You can put off answering if you believe that the question will be answered later in the session and say so. But meet each question squarely; even if it is loaded, you need to deal with it.

4. *Do not engage in put downs.* Many questions may seem simple, even unnecessary to you. Remember, however, that the learners had reasons for asking them, so do not be condescending.

Special Kinds of Questions

You can expect to face a full gamut of human nature and behaviors in your role as a trainer. You probably will have to deal with many questions that you will wish had not been asked. The following are a few samples and tips for dealing with them.

1. *Irrelevant* questions that do not relate to the topic may be an indication of boredom or of a learner who is having difficulty. The intent may be to sidetrack the session. Sometimes it is best just to state politely that the question is not appropriate and proceed. Another possibility is to use the active listening technique to try to discover the actual problem.

2. If you have inadvertently contradicted yourself, a learner may decide to nail you for it. This is called a "gotcha" question. The best response in this case is to admit your mistake (if there actually was one) and move on.

3. If you realize that the asker is using a question to achieve something else—such as attempting to disagree with a concept that already has been accepted by everyone else—one approach is to rephrase the question into a more legitimate one.

4. There is a type of question that indicates that the asker has missed one (or more) major points and

may be lost. The dilemma is that if you stop to bring that person up to speed, you may be punishing the others; but to continue the lesson may cause you to completely lose the one person. If you decide to move on, be sure to agree to help the confused person later.

USING STRUCTURED EXPERIENCES

Structured experiences get learners involved in doing something other than sitting and listening. They employ the concept of experiential learning, that is, the learners do whatever action is required and gain something (knowledge, experience, insight, etc.) as a result of the experience.

There are many types of structured experiences, and there are many sources of ones that have been tested and proved successful. Many of these are listed in the selected references at the end of this chapter. Structured experiences can range from very light activities to very complex tasks or simulations. Some are designed purely to loosen up the group or to introduce the members to one another. Other structured experiences can be used to emphasize concepts, such as the importance of two-way communication or the problems associated with reaching consensus in a group. These experiences become integral parts of the learning process.

The important thing to remember in using structured experiences is that the learning is more important than the activity that is used to get it across. The activity chosen should be relevant to the learning goals and should stimulate discussion of what the experience meant or taught to the learners.[8] Merely introducing a "game" is not enough; it is in encouraging the *learners* to discuss what happened, what that meant, and how these learnings can be applied that you will utilize the full value of this training tool. If you

---

[8]An excellent discussion of the use of experiential learning is found in the "Introduction to the Structured Experiences Section" in J.W. Pfeiffer and J.E. Jones (Eds.), *The 1980 Annual Handbook for Group Facilitators,* San Diego, CA: University Associates, 1980.

do not allow the learners to validate their own experiences, you have merely run a demonstration and given a lecture.

ADDITIONAL TRAINING TECHNOLOGIES

There are several additional techniques for getting learners involved. As you become more experienced as a trainer, you probably will use a variety of these and combine them. Some of them are:

Tests. Tests not only help to measure progress and provide feedback, but also provide a means of getting the learners to participate.

Instruments. Also called data-feedback devices or inventories, these paper-and-pencil response forms do *not* *test* what a learner knows, they collect data for the learners to use. If the instrument is personal in focus, the data may be on one's preferred style of dealing with conflict, one's need for power, and so on. There are no right or wrong answers from these inventories; they merely are a means for obtaining information to be used in the training. Many instruments are backed up by research studies that validate the way in which the questions are asked and the responses interpreted.

Trainer/Learner-Developed Materials. Taking notes is one form of this. Another is to have work sheets for the learners to complete at various times during the session. If the lesson involves some sort of problem solving, you can have the learners work sample problems.

Demonstration. Never demonstrate something that a learner can demonstrate for you. This may be true even if you have to tell the person how to do everything. Getting at least one person involved has a positive effect on the others.

Presentations/Recitations. This is the technique of having learners stand up (or sit down) and explain the whys, whats, and hows of something. For the time, they become co-trainers. Have them, after advanced preparation, present new materials to the group. Make sure that you use as many learners as possible during the course of the training; do not concentrate on one or two only.

Active Listening. This technique also can be used to get learners involved.

Case Studies. Case studies require the learners to react with solutions to problems that are depicted in the cases. This method is used extensively in business schools and in the behavioral sciences. If you can use case studies in your training situation, do so. It is an excellent way to get people to think and to respond.

Simulations/Games. This method is typified by the flight simulators that are used by the military and the airlines to train pilots. Some driver-training courses use driving simulators. Simulators range from relatively simple, game-like devices to complex electronic/digital computers. The less sophisticated (and less expensive) ones are similar to popular board games. They teach such things as strategy, negotiation, and decision making. These are frequently used in management training. They may require several people to interact with one another or can be designed for use by an individual. Simulations are very specialized and will mean extra effort if you decide to use them.

Role Playing. Total immersion in the learning process can be achieved by using a role play. This technique is used commonly in teaching human relations skills and in sales training. If done with enthusiasm, it is an effective means of learning. Role plays may be highly structured, with the roles well defined, or they may allow the people who are playing the roles a great deal of flexibility in acting them out.

In using any of these technologies, it is important to have specific objectives and guidelines. Whatever is demonstrated and ultimately learned should contribute to the achievement of the specific learning objectives of the training session.

If your learning requirements involve a physical object such as a machine or tools of any sort, try to make the learning environment as nearly like an actual work situation as possible—and include all the safety precautions that would be present in the work place.

SUMMARY

Attaining maximum involvement of learners in the learning process is one of the greatest objectives of a training facilitator. People learn best by doing. This should be kept in mind during the planning design of the training as well as in the actual conduct of training. The use of a variety of experiential techniques will enhance the learning process. There are numerous ways to get learners involved.

Some of the key points from this chapter are:

● The use of questions is one of the best means available to stimulate learner response.

● Questions help to arouse interest, stimulate thinking, keep the training on track, and obtain vital feedback.

● Open-ended questions are preferable because they require thought and reasoning, and some of this usually is evidenced in the answers given.

SELECTED REFERENCES

Before using any training technology that is new to you, study it thoroughly until you are comfortable with it and know how to use it, and make sure it is suitable—adapted if necessary—to your situation. Most of the following references contain material on using and adapting experiential learning designs.

Communications Research Associates. *A workbook for interpersonal communication* (2nd ed.). Dubuque, IA: Kendall/ Hunt, 1978.

Craig, R.L. (Ed.). *Training and development handbook* (2nd ed.). New York: McGraw-Hill, 1976. (Includes chapters on role playing, laboratory training, programmed instruction, simulation, and learner-controlled instruction.)

Davies, I.K. *Instructional technique.* New York: McGraw-Hill, 1981.

Davis, L.N. *Planning, conducting, and evaluating workshops.* San Diego, CA: Learning Concepts, 1974.

Gaw, B.A. Processing questions: An aid to completing the learning cycle. In J.E. Jones & J.W. Pfeiffer (Eds.), *The 1979 annual handbook for group facilitators.* San Diego, CA: University Associates, 1979.

Hutson, H., & Dormant, D. The name of the game is frame. *Training,* April, 1981, 54-56.

Knowles, M. *Self-directed learning.* Chicago: Follett, 1975.

Maier, N.R.F., Solem, A.R., & Maier, A.A. *The role-play technique: A handbook for management and leadership practice.* San Diego, CA: University Associates, 1975.

Newstrom, J.W., & Scannel, E.E. *Games trainers play.* New York: McGraw-Hill, 1980.

Pfeiffer, J.W., & Goodstein, L. (Eds.). *The 1982 annual for facilitators, trainers, and consultants.* San Diego, CA: University Associates, 1982.

Pfeiffer, J.W., Heslin, R., & Jones, J.E. *Instrumentation in human relations training* (2nd ed.). San Diego, CA: University Associates, 1976.

Pfeiffer, J.W., & Jones, J.E. (Eds.), *A handbook of structured experiences for human relations training* (8 vols.). San Diego, CA: University Associates, 1969-1981.

Pfeiffer, J.W., & Jones, J.E. (Eds.). *The annual handbook for group facilitators* (10 vols.). San Diego, CA: University Associates, 1972-1981.

(The University Associates books offer over three hundred structured experiences organized into specific categories, with complete instructions for how to use them, in addition to instruments, role plays, and other training tools.)

Randall, J.S. You and effective training—Part 9: The art of questioning. *Training and Development Journal,* December, 1978, 27-31.

Shaw, M.E., Corsini, R.J., Blake, R.R., & Mouton, J.S. *Role playing: A practical manual for group facilitators.* San Diego, CA: University Associates, 1980.

ANSWERS TO EXERCISE ON PAGE 138

1. Taken literally, the answer would be either yes or no. Ask the question more directly: "How did the word barbecue originate?"

2. Too many thoughts are grouped together. Also, the answers to the second two parts of the question may help to answer the first part. Break it down into three separate questions. As the answers are given, find new questions (even direct ones) to tie the answers together.

3. There is no way of knowing if any answer could be related to the performance you are looking for from the learner. The question must be more explicit, such as "Name three reasons for using audiovisual aids in a classroom setting." Answers to this question then can be rephrased as open-ended questions, such as "Why is reason A effective?"

4. This is another case in which the literal answer is either yes or no. An open-ended way to ask this is: "Why are closed-ended questions less effective than open-ended ones?"

5. The answer to this will not tell you much. The question could be broken down into two questions: (a) "What are the methods for determining whether or not a learner understands a given concept?" followed by (b) "When would you use each method?"

Chapter 12
Control and Group Dynamics

Group behavior is a melting pot of the behaviors of all the members of the group. Understanding and maintaining control of group behavior is necessary for the trainer.

When you have completed this chapter, you will be able to:

- state the elements of group dynamics,
- identify the types of group behavior,
- initiate control procedures in various group situations.

We all have learned a lot about group behavior simply by being members of so many different groups—work groups, ethnic groups, religious groups, social groups, family groups, service groups, and so on. We know that groups take on unique personalities of their own, have problems, and work through them. We have experienced the processes of determining who will emerge as the leader of the group, what associations will be formed among the members, and so on. Group behavior also has been studied by social psychologists, educational psychologists, and many others, and consistently recurring patterns have been observed. These are referred to as group dynamics, and the use of the word "dynamics" indicates the development and change that occurs over the life of any but the most temporary group.

In the training situation, you may be part of a group for only an hour or you may help to create the group and take it though several days (or longer) of experience. Either way, a very basic knowledge of group dynamics (and how to deal with problem situations) is a tool that you will learn to appreciate.

ELEMENTS OF GROUPS

Purpose

Most groups are formed for a specific purpose (even if it is just to have a good time). In a training group, however, individuals are brought together to pursue (albeit the same type of) individual learning goals. The reason for a group in this case generally is that it is more economical to teach people that way. The more individualized and self-paced the instruction is, the fewer group dynamics there are. For this discussion, however, it is assumed that the group members do interact and, thus, that relationships and reactions will occur. In addition, there are elements of group life that can enhance the learning process.

Norms

Every group has standards or values, ways in which they do things or view things. Knowing the norms of the group can aid in understanding the learners in the group. It may be easy to discern what the norms are if you are training a group of senior computer scientists who work together and who all are members of the Association for Computing Machinery. In contrast, a computer class in a community college is likely to consist of a range of people, from students who are there because it was the only class they could get, to people who want to change their jobs, or to people who take courses just for the learning experience.

Structure

Group structure can be formal or informal. Training classes tend to be formal. Yet, informality—especially with a group of motivated adults—can make the training more enjoyable and less stressful. A good rule is to try to achieve a happy medium. The more formal the procedures and resulting atmosphere, the greater will be the control that the trainer can exert. Of course, if the learning process runs smoothly, the trainer need not pay much attention to the issue of control.

Roles

The most important role in a group is the role of leader. Some of the others are joker (which can be either good or bad), silent member (which is not good for learning), protagonist, scapegoat, expert, and so on. The roles chosen will depend on the personalities in the group. Well-prepared and well-presented criterion-referenced instruction can overcome almost any of the problems that might arise as a result of member roles.

Leadership

Someone in a group almost always will attempt to assume the role of leader, and this is natural. In a training group, although the trainer is the key leader, encouraging class leaders to emerge from among the learners can have a positive influence on the training-learning process. The degree and type of leadership that the trainer will need to exercise will depend on the purpose and nature of the group.

Effectiveness

In a training situation, this is primarily an individual matter. Fortunately, in most cases (unless it is a decision about where to go for lunch), you will not have to worry about reaching joint decisions and solutions to problems other than in a case-study mode. If specific learning tasks and performance objectives are involved, effectiveness will be simple to determine.

Communication

Communication is a primary consideration and (problem) for most groups. It is multiplied by the number of people in the group. Not only must the trainer communicate effectively with each person, but all the others are listening when any two people are sending and receiving messages. Effective communication between learners contributes to the total learning process.

GROUP BEHAVIORS

Group behavior is comprised of the collective behaviors of all the members of the group, as well as the natural flow of group processes that are common to all groups. In the beginning, the group tends to depend on and follow the leader while the members sort out their relationships and tasks. Once this is done, some friction may develop as the group "organizes" itself with regard to member roles, influence, and expertise. In the third stage, people begin to feel a sense of belonging and begin to share. Members may tell jokes and enjoy the less stressful atmosphere. Finally, the group members turn their attention to the group's task. Problem solving and communication are effective. Although they have a feeling of mutuality, the group members now can work well collectively or individually. The interpersonal dimension being pretty well settled, the members now have the time, energy, and support to concentrate on achieving their goals. This process is aided if the members begin with group-oriented behavior. Problem behaviors on the part of one or two members can greatly hinder the development of the group.

MEMBER BEHAVIORS

The types of member behaviors can be classed according to three categories:

- task-directed,
- maintenance,

- self-centered.

The book by Davis (1974) that is referenced at the end of this chapter provides brief, excellent coverage of this subject. The first two categories of behavior are productive; the third is not. In the training setting, a task behavior is one that helps to move the learning process along. A maintenance behavior would be one that helps to maintain positive relations among the group members.

For each of the three types of individual behaviors within a group, there are numerous examples of specific behaviors. Figure 13 lists some of them. Which behaviors should be encouraged and which should be discouraged will be obvious.

Productive

Task-Directed Behaviors	Maintenance Behaviors
Initiating/contributing	Encouraging
Information seeking/giving	Harmonizing
Opinion seeking/giving	Compromising
Elaborating	Including
Coordinating	Observing process
Orienting	Following
Evaluating	
Moving/shaking	
Recording	

Unproductive

Self-Centered Behaviors

Being aggressive
Seeking recognition
Dominating
Pleading for a special interest
Blocking
Playing
Crying on others' shoulders

From *Introduction to Group Dynamics* by Malcolm S. Knowles, Copyright © 1972 by Association Press/Follett. Used by permission of Follett Publishing Company.

Figure 13. Typical Group-Member Behaviors

CONTROL

Training-group members will respond individually as well as collectively as a group. Dealing with the wide variety of individual personalities is a challenging experience even for the seasoned trainer. There are three types of members who tend to require more control on the part of the trainer:

- those who say nothing,
- those who want to do all the talking,
- those who want to get off the subject at hand.

If the silent person learns little, the training has not done its job. If the monopolizer succeeds, the training definitely has not done its job. There are things that you can do to exert influence on these behaviors.[9]

Silent Individuals

The possible reasons for this behavior are lack of interest or motivation, lack of understanding, feelings on the part of the silent members that they cannot make a contribution or feelings that they do not belong, or the fact that they are slow thinkers or that they just do not like to talk. Look for ways to get these people to contribute but do not force the issue. Above all, do not accuse these people of not saying enough.

Monopolizers

The possible reasons for this behavior are that that these people truly know more than the others, want to help, are enthusiastic and impatient to move on, or have "know-it-all" personalities, want to be the group leaders, or have strong needs for recognition. Establish impartiality and an

---

[9]This discussion is based largely on John S. Randall, "You and Effective Thinking," Parts 7 and 8: "Instructor Conduct/Control," *Training and Development Journal*, November, 1978, pages 54-60. Reprinted by permission of the author.

"equal-time" norm in the beginning of the group's life and stick to it. Let other members of group take care of this type of person or recognize this person's contribution and then call on someone else, before the monopolizer has the chance to speak again.

Side Trackers

The possible reasons for this type of behavior are that the individuals in question do not understand the group's objectives, want to avoid the topic, cannot concentrate because of emotions, or want other information. Make the objectives clear. Politely tell these people that their questions are beyond the scope of the lesson, but that you will attempt to answer the question during the break. Keep coming back to the main point of the discussion. Then, during the next break period, you can attempt to identify the reason for the question and can deal with it.

At all times, the trainer must respect the members of the group as individuals. Their reasons for acting as they do are valid to them. Recognize this and deal with the situation accordingly, but *never* denigrate any member of the group. To do so could kill any chance you ever had of helping that person to learn.

Using Assertion

Assertion training is very popular these days, if one can judge by the number of workshops and training materials that exist on the topic. Being assertive means standing up for your rights, but not at the expense of the rights of others. One of the things that works in training to control a problem learner is to keep repeating your answer. For example, if a learner is insistent on varying the flow of the lesson, each time the point is made, your answer would be a variation of "No, we are not going to change." After hearing the same, steady answer over and over, the member eventually will get the point or give up.

TEAM BUILDING

Team building is a process of developing a group of people who work together for the purpose of contributing positively to the goals of the team. Even though training is largely an individual effort, making a positive impact on the group's dynamics can make a corresponding contribution to the learning process. Thus, some of the techniques of team building can be useful in the training environment. Even if the group of learners will be together for just a day or two, it is to everyone's benefit if all work together toward achieving the learning objectives. The following are some tips taken from pactical applications of team building.

- Make sure that people get acquainted with one another. (Chapter 11 will give you some ideas about this.)
- Allow some time for the learners who display positive behaviors to establish their roles. Over a period of time, this will be a natural occurence, but be sure to encourage such behaviors.
- Encourage the members to engage in social activities such as having meals together. If most people are from out of town, there will be more opportunity for this.
- Encourage the members to engage in recreational activities together. A jog during the noon break or a tennis game after the last session of the day can help to establish good rapport.
- Give the group problems to solve in order to allow the members to work together.

EXERCISE

This exercise deals with group behavior. If you are not currently in an instructional setting, choose one of the groups of which you currently are a member and use it as the basis for your answers. Using the aspects of group dynamics outlined in this chapter, analyze your group or organization, making observations on the following:

1. The norms of the group—what values and expectations does it have?

2. Are the norms cohesive or individually diverse?

3. Is the structure formal or informal?

4. What would happen if the structure were the other way?

5. What are the various roles that people fill?

6. Who fills them and how do they do it?

7. Who exercises leadership?

8. How effective is the group in doing what it is supposed to do?

9. Describe the main communication processes in the group.

10. Do these processes work?

Add more questions as you think of them. Use what you learn about group dynamics in this study group when you become part of other groups.

SUMMARY

Some knowledge of group dynamics, of group process, can help the trainer to deal with learner groups. Knowledge of the group's norms, structure, emerging leadership, and communications can be used to promote task-oriented and maintenance behaviors and to avoid self-centered member behaviors. The trainer must deal quickly with those learners (such as silent individuals, monopolizers, and side-trackers) who behave in a way that is detrimental to the learning process.

SELECTED REFERENCES

Many references on group dynamics and behavior exist, including those that are based in psychology. Here are several easy-to-follow references.

Bradford, L.P. (Ed.). *Group development* (2nd ed.). San Diego, CA: University Associates, 1978.

Davis, L.N. *Planning, conducting, and evaluating workshops.* San Diego, CA: Learning Concepts, 1974.

Dyer, W.G. *Team building: Issues and alternatives.* Reading, MA: Addison-Wesley, 1977.

Jones, J.E. Dealing with disruptive individuals in meetings. In J.W. Pfeiffer & J.E. Jones (Eds.), *The 1980 annual handbook for group facilitators.* San Diego, CA: University Associates, 1980.

Kelley, C. *Assertion training: A facilitator's guide.* San Diego, CA: University Associates, 1979.

Knowles, M., & Knowles, H. *Introduction to group dynamics* (2nd ed.). Chicago: Association Press/Follett, 1972.

Randall, J.S. You and effective training (Parts 7 and 8: Instructor conduct/control). *Training and Development Journal,* November, 1978, 54-60.

Reilly, A.J., & Jones, J.E. Team building. In J.W. Pfeiffer & J.E. Jones (Eds.), *The 1974 annual handbook for group facilitators.* San Diego, CA: University Associates, 1974.

PART IV
EVALUATION OF TRAINING

Chapter 13
Evaluation of Training

Evaluating everything about a training session—your performance, the learners' performances, and the training itself—is a difficult but necessary step of the training cycle.

When you have completed this chapter, you will be able to:

- identify the various types of evaluation that must be performed,
- identify when each evaluation should be conducted,
- perform at least the basic steps of the various types of evaluation.

When the last learner has left the training area, the last part of the trainer's job is just beginning. Now is the time to perform the step that completes the training cycle: the *evaluation.* Although it is not the most enjoyable part of the training function, evaluation could well be the most important.

WHY EVALUATE?

Training is a very dynamic process. Its elements cannot be left for long without the possibility of their becoming stagnant, outdated, or inaccurate—perhaps even harmful to the learning effort. Subject matter changes continually in training situations, and trainers develop lazy habits. In addition, learners do not always learn precisely what the training was intended to teach them. These are but a few of the reasons why every training effort must be evaluated. Evaluation closes the loop of the training process (see Figure 14).

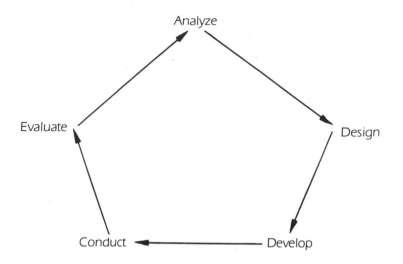

Figure 14. The Training Cycle As a Closed-Loop, Continuous System

TYPES OF EVALUATION

Evaluation can be divided into three types, although they do overlap and all three are required to provide effective evaluation. The three types are: self-evaluation, learner evaluation, and testing.

Self-Evaluation. This is the process of determining how effective you are as a trainer. You need to do your own evaluation, but critique from observers can be helpful.

Learner Evaluation. This is the process in which the learners express their opinions and make observations about the effectiveness of the training.

Testing. This is the process of determining whether or not the learners learned what was intended. It can be done informally, with questions, or by means of various types of written or performance tests.

Don Kirkpatrick, an authority in the field of training

evaluation, has divided the subject into four broad segments:[10]

1. Measuring the *reactions* of participants—how well they liked the training.
2. Measuring the *learning* of knowledge, skills, and attitudes.
3. Measuring on-the-job *behavioral* changes that result from the training.
4. Measuring desired *results*. Were they achieved?

Measuring the fourth aspect, results, is extremely difficult to do.

Self-Evaluation

It usually is difficult for people to critique themselves, but one way to obtain the maximum information is to do your evaluation shortly after each session has ended and again shortly after the entire training workshop or course has ended. In this way, you will best be able to remember what you did and said, the reactions of the learners, and any problems that occurred to you. Not only will you benefit professionally from your self-evaluation, but in the end, it is the learners who will benefit most and, after all, that is what training is all about.

A Self-Evaluation Check List

The purpose of the check list in Figure 15 is to help you to perform self-evaluation. After you answer each of the questions, you will have an excellent idea of how things went and, more importantly, how to prepare for the next session.

If the word "will" is substituted for "did" in the self-evaluation check list, the list becomes a tool of a different sort; it becomes a planning guide.

---

[10]Copyright © 1975, *Training and Development Journal,* American Society for Training and Development. Reprinted with permission. All rights reserved.

Material

1. Was my material appropriate for the group?
2. Was it well organized?
3. Did I make the objectives known?
4. Did I explain and emphasize main points?
5. Did I achieve the objectives?
6. Were my communication aids effective?
7. Were my handouts adequate?
8. Did I summarize?
9. Were the case studies or problems of value?

Presentation

1. Did I secure the attention and interest of the group members?
2. Did I give a coherent presentation?
3. Did I motivate the group?
4. Did I use my communication aids effectively?
5. Did I establish rapport with the group?
6. Did I encourage participation?
7. Did I use simple, understandable, correct language?
8. Did I use the proper tone of voice?
9. Were my gestures meaningful?
10. Did I say "ah" or "er" or use words such as "well" or "now" excessively?
11. Could I be heard and understood?
12. Did I use proper questioning techniques?
13. Was my demonstration correct and well organized?
14. Did I make the best use of the time available?

Facilities

1. Were the physical arrangements satisfactory?
2. Did I keep adequate records?

Post-Course

1. Were the training objectives achieved? To what degree? If not, why not?
2. Were the learner's expectations met? How do I know?
3. What were some of the indications of changes in knowledge, skills, or attitudes?
4. What training methods worked well? Why? Which ones were not successful? Why?

Figure 15. Trainer Self-Evaluation Check List

Figure 15 (continued)

5. Were the facilities and equipment satisfactory? How might they be improved?
6. What improvements can be made in the material?
7. Did everyone participate?
8. Did I stimulate discussion?

Source: John S. Randall, *Training and Development Journal,* December, 1978, page 31. Copyright © 1978, *Training and Development Journal,* American Society for Training and Development. Reprinted with permission. All rights reserved.

One final note on self-evaluation: it leads to improvement. That is important. While you critique what could be improved in your performance, look for the good things that you did, too. Then keep repeating them as long as they work.

Learner Evaluation

There are two times when you can sense how well you are performing in conducting training: when you do extremely well and when you do extremely badly. Most training experiences are likely to fall somewhere in between. Therefore, it behooves you to seek the opinions of others. Perhaps another trainer can sit in the back of the room and observe. Such a critique, especially when done by an experienced trainer, is a valuable input for you.

Another source of constructive criticism is readily available: the learners. And it is a safe bet that they are willing, even eager, to have their say. Seek and use this valuable source of evaluative information.

Learner Evaluation Forms

Many learner evaluation forms exist. The type that you will use will depend on your training situation. Some of the things that you want to receive feedback on are as follows:

- How useful was the material for the learners' jobs?
- How do the learners rate your training performance and qualifications?
- Were the learning objectives understood?
- What was the value of the audiovisual (and other) training aids that were used?
- How effective was the allocation of time (overall and various segments)?
- Were the facilities adequate?
- How do the learners rate the helpfulness and attitude of the trainers?
- Were the learners satisfied with the flow of the training event?
- What suggestions do the learners have for improvement?

A typical evaluation form is shown in Figure 16. This form is not too tedious to fill out and it is easy to follow. Use such a form at the end of a training course or at the juncture of a major segment. It is all right to use one at the end of a lesson for the first time or two that the lesson is used or if revision of the lesson is being considered, but do not overdo such use.

LEARNER COURSE EVALUATION   Date _____

Your Name _____ Your Job Title _____

Course _____ Trainer _____

Please respond to each item. Your written comments are helpful and welcome. Please try to be specific.

What might we add to or delete from the course to increase its usefulness?

Figure 16. Sample Training Evaluation Form

Figure 16 (continued)

Please respond below (left to right): disagree strongly, disagree, uncertain, agree, agree strongly).

How Do You Feel About:

1. The course content is useful for my job.

Comment: _____

2. The instructor shows strong technical knowledge of the subject.

Comment: _____

3. The course topics were sequenced logically.

Comment: _____

4. The course's objectives were explained clearly.

Comment: _____

5. The trainer's presentation was well paced and clear.

Comment: _____

6. The visual instructional aids helped me to learn.

Comment: _____

Figure 16 (continued)

7. The course handouts are useful
   reference material for me.

   Comment: _____

8. The problems presented for me to
   solve were useful learning
   experiences.

   Comment: _____

9. The time allocation of the course
   was adequate for me.

   Comment: _____

10. The trainer answered my questions
    thoroughly.

    Comment: _____

11. The trainer gave me adequate
    individual help with my problems.

    Comment: _____

12. The training facilities were adequate
    and comfortable.

    Comment: _____

Testing

The training in which you are involved may or may not involve testing. If not, it is a good idea to have at least an informal summary and question or discussion session, in order to determine if the learning is "on track," i.e., whether or not the learning objectives have been met by each learner. If these were clearly established prior to the start of the training, such an evaluation should be relatively easy.

Types of Tests

Tests can be devised to measure both performance and knowledge.

Performance tests. These tests measure skills. The learner must demonstrate the ability to do something such as operate a device, fly an airplane, or speak a foreign language. In some cases, simulation can be used. At other times, it may be necessary to devise a test that requires a performance that is equivalent to the one desired but not exactly the same. The particular nature of any performance test will depend on the subject matter to be tested, the available resources, and other factors.

Knowledge tests. There are two types of knowledge tests: subjective and objective. Subjective, or essay, tests are not ordinarily used in training situations, especially when the training is criterion referenced. In part, this is because standardization and grading present difficulties with this type of test.

There are several types of objective tests:

- oral,
- true/false,
- multiple choice,
- matching,
- completion (fill in the blanks).

All of these have application in evaluating knowledge learning. Care must be taken in constructing these types of tests. Although detailed information on how to prepare objective knowledge tests are beyond the scope of this chapter, Table 5 lists some helpful hints for constructing and using them, and the selected references at the end of this chapter contain a number of books that deal specifically with test construction and use.

Tests can be administered any time that you feel they will help—before the lesson starts, during the lesson, or after. The reasons for testing are essentially the same as the reasons for asking questions.

Table 5. Considerations in Developing Objective Tests

Considerations for Various Types of Tests

Type	Do	Do Not
True/False	Use good grammar; use short, clear sentences.	Use tricks; have obvious patterns; use negatives; have questions linked together.
Multiple Choice	Give four or five alternatives; make most alternatives plausible; give consistent choices.	Have obvious patterns; use "none" or "all of the above."
Matching	Use five to ten items; give more answers than questions; have everything relevant.	
Completion	Place blanks near the end of items; require a single idea per blank.	Have statements copied directly; have blanks at the beginning of an item; omit verbs; use many blanks; give clues by the length of the blanks.

Table 5 (continued)

Steps in Test Construction

1. Determine the scope of the test.
2. Determine what is to be measured.
3. Select the test items.
4. Select the technique.
5. Determine the length of the test.
6. Make the final selection of test items.
7. Arrange the items in final form.
8. Prepare the directions for taking the test.
9. Prepare the scoring device.
10. Question the questions.

From *Test Construction for Training Evaluation* by Charles C. Denova. Copyright © 1979 by Van Nostrand Reinhold Company. Reprinted by permission of the publisher.

SUMMARY

Evaluation is a continuing process that completes the closed-loop training system. Some of the key points concerning evaluation are:

- The three basic types of training evalution are trainer self-evaluation, learner evaluation, and tests.
- Evaluation helps to demonstrate whether or not the learning objectives have been achieved.
- Written forms assist in the process of evaluation.
- Objective tests are most suitable for learner evaluation in training situations.

SELECTED REFERENCES

The publications *Training* (731 Hennepin Avenue, Minneapolis, Minnesota 55403) and *Training and Development Journal* (American Society for Training and Development, 600 Maryland Avenue S.W., Washington, DC 20024) regularly publish articles on testing and evaluation.

Briggs, L.J. (Ed.). *Instructional design.* Engelwood Cliffs, NJ: Educational Technology Publications, 1972.

Craig, R.L. (Ed.). *Training and development handbook* (2nd ed.). New York: McGraw-Hill, 1976.

Denova, C.C. *Test construction for training evaluation.* New York: Van Nostrand Reinhold, 1979.

Kirkpatrick, D.L. (Ed.). *Evaluating training programs.* Washington, DC: American Society for Training and Development, 1975.

Mager, R.F. *Measuring instructional intent.* Belmont, CA: Fearon-Pitman, 1973.

PART V
REVIEW

Chapter 14
Review of Book

A trainer has the potential of functioning in a wide variety of roles, calling on many different skills and talents. Regardless of where you are and what you do, there are certain attributes that can help you to become a successful facilitator of learning.

When you have completed this chapter, you will be able to:

- state a number of attributes of the successful trainer,
- identify key points from the previous thirteen chapters in this book.

This closing chapter has two purposes. One is to summarize what has been covered in this book. The other is to point out a number of attributes of successful trainers. Looking back at what you have learned is a great way to reinforce the learning. Just as you follow this adage in your training pursuits, so, too, will we follow it here.

THE TRAINING CYCLE

The five phases of the training cycle, or system, are presented again in Figure 20. As a trainer, you might be called on to perform only one or two phases for a given training event. This is not *unusual*; however, to be most effective, each trainer should be part of a total systems approach to training. The five phases are:

1. *Analyze* to determine training requirements. This makes sure that training is needed, then makes sure it is geared to the right need.

173

2. *Design* the training approach. This leads to the best (most effective and cost efficient) strategy of training for the purpose you have identified. It includes identifying the learning objectives, the most appropriate training approach and media, any prerequisites for learners, and the length of time required to complete the training.

3. *Develop* the training materials. This includes fleshing out the course outline and arranging for lesson plans, learner materials, audiovisual aids, evaluation sheets, physical arrangements, time sequencing, and trainer briefing.

4. *Conduct* the training. This involves applying the analyzed, designed, and developed materials to the learners in the form of a course, workshop, or other training session and keeping track of how things are going as you do so.

5. *Evaluate* and update the training. This is what you do to ensure that the training is always the best that it can be. This is the step that closes the loop. It includes trainer evaluation, learner evaluation, and whatever additional evaluation is appropriate and possible.

How the materials in the previous thirteen chapters fit into the five phases of the training cycle also is shown in Figure 17.

THE TRAINER'S ROLE

The personal characteristics that contribute positively to the role of facilitator include:
- being organized,
- being over prepared,
- showing empathy,
- being patient,
- being enthusiastic,
- giving positive feedback.

To be effective, all training activities must be coordinated parts of the total training process—analyzing, designing, developing, conducting, and evaluating. Individual training tasks, such as writing a curriculum or facilitating a half-day workshop, should be done within the context of the total process. A design task must be based on sound analysis, a development task must be based on sound design, and evaluation must be fed back into the process all along the way.

	Chapter	Analyze	Design	Develop	Conduct	Evaluate
1	What is Training?	X	X	X	X	X
2	The Roles of the Trainer	X	X	X	X	X
3	Learning Theory		X	X	X	
4	Getting Started			X	X	
5	Preparing Learning Objectives and Lesson Plans			X	X	
6	Using Audiovisual Aids			X	X	
7	Interpersonal Communication				X	
8	Active Listening				X	X
9	Transactional Analysis As a Communication Tool				X	
10	Motivating Learners				X	
11	Getting People Involved				X	
12	Control and Group Dynamics		X			
13	Evaluation of Training					X

Figure 17. The Relationship Between Chapter Material and the Five Phases of Training

MORE ON CHECK LISTS

Early in this book, the value of check lists was stated. Training is a lot like piloting a 747—there are just too many things to do before, during, and afterwards to rely on memory alone. This is why check lists are so important.

CHAPTER HIGHLIGHTS

The recommended way to review these chapters is to go through them again, possibly rereading portions, going over the summaries at the ends of the chapters, and also noting the figures, which are designed to highlight key points. The following are the key points of each of the previous thirteen chapters.

Chapter	Key Points
1 What Is Training?	• Training is a closed-loop system. • The five phases of training are: analyze, design, develop, conduct, and evaluate. • Training should have clearly stated learning objectives. • There are many types of training, from classroom to role playing. • The learner has the ultimate responsibility for learning.
2 The Roles of the Trainer	• Flexibility is important. • The trainer is both a manager and an operator. • Some critical trainer roles are subject-matter expert, counselor, leader/motivator, psychologist, manager, and human being.

Chapter	Key Points
3 Learning Theory	• The trainer's key role is to facilitate learning. • The three types of learning are cognitive (knowledge), psychomotor (physical), and affective (attitude). • Several practices promote learning; these are: stating the learning objectives, practice, giving guidance and prompting, giving and soliciting feedback, encouraging transfer of learning, using related activities, and appearing competent and enthusiastic. • Adults are different; they learn because they choose to learn; they want to become involved; the material must be relevant to them; they relate their learning to their existing knowledge; and they should be treated as peers. • Repetition helps the memory process.
4 Getting Started	• Every hour of training presentation requires at least three hours of preparation. • The learners should be given some information in advance of the training. • Check lists are helpful and necessary.

Chapter	Key Points
4 (continued)	• The physical facilities and schedule can have an effect on the learning process. • The appearance of the trainer is important. • The first few minutes set the stage for the rest of the event.
5 Preparing Learning Objectives and Lesson Plans	• Learning objectives provide criteria for designing, developing, conducting, and evaluating training. • Objectives must be precise, be measurable, and employ action words. • The full objective states the performance to be achieved, the conditions under which it will be done, and the standard for the performance. • A lesson plan is essential to guide each training session.
6 Using Audiovisual Aids	• Audiovisual aids highlight, reinforce, and add variety to learning. • A wide variety of aids and media is available. • The most commonly used medium in training is the overhead projector. • Visual aids must be relevant and easy to understand.
7 Interpersonal Communication	• Interpersonal communication is a closed-loop, two-way process.

Chapter	Key Points
7 (continued)	• The elements of the communication process are: sender, receiver, message, and channel. • Simplicity is one key to successful communication. • Feedback is essential. • Nonverbal communication is very important.
8 Active Listening	• Active listening consists of feeding back what you think the speaker said, rather than commenting on it. • Active listening is means of encouraging the learner to communicate more freely and is helpful in problem solving. • Showing empathy encourages nondefensive communication.
9 Transactional Analysis As a Communication Tool	• Transactional analysis is a means of deciding the basis from which the other person is communicating or interacting. • People live according to life scripts in which they play the roles of parent, adult, or child. • The adult mode is the most effective. • If a person is speaking as an adult, communication is hampered if the person is not responded to as an adult. • Most people want and need positive strokes.

Chapter	Key Points
10 Motivating Learners	• There are two classes of motivation: physiological and psychological. • Motivated behavior is directed toward achieving something; it is selective; and it can be satisfied. • Motivation to learn is influenced, in part, by natural curiosity, the need to achieve, the desire to be with others, and the attraction of the power that knowledge and skill can bring. • McGregor says that a humanitarian, rather than authoritarian, approach works best with people. • Maslow charted a hierarchy of needs that range from basic physical needs to self-actualization. • Herzberg says that motivator factors make people work and hygiene factors help to maintain performance.
11 Getting People Involved	• Learner involvement is vital to the learning process. • Questioning is one of best methods for getting learners involved; questions stimulate thinking, provide feedback, and help to keep the learners on track.

Chapter	Key Points
11 (continued)	• Open-ended questions are best because they reveal the thoughts behind the answers. • Structured experiences, tests, instruments, case studies, and other training technologies also can be used to stimulate learner involvement in the learning process.
12 Control and Group Dynamics	• Group behavior is comprised of the behaviors of the individual members and the natural development of group dynamics. • Elements that influence groups are: purpose, norms, structure, roles, leadership, effectiveness, and communication. • Stages of group dynamics include: following the leader, organizing roles and influence, belonging and sharing, and problem solving and goal achievement. • Task-directed and maintenance behaviors are conducive to a good learning environment. • The trainer must act promptly to include silent members and deal with monopolizers and side trackers before these behaviors can negatively affect the learning environment.

Chapter	Key Points
12 (continued)	• Encouraging team-building activities helps to develop positive group behavior.
13 Evaluation of Training	• Evaluation is essential; it closes the loop of the training cycle. • Without evaluation, training can become stagnant or outdated. • The three types of evaluation are: trainer self-evaluation, learner evaluation, and testing. • Check lists and evaluation forms are useful and valuable tools. • Testing can measure knowledge or performance; the type of test that is most appropriate depends on the nature of the learning.

In short, the basic tenets of training to be extracted from this book are:

1. *Be prepared.*
2. The primary *role* of the trainer is to *facilitate* the learning process.
3. *Show enthusiasm.*
4. *Close the loop* with feedback in any form of communication.
5. *Ask questions.*
6. *Define the learning criteria* and base the learning process on these objectives.
7. *Get the learners involved.*
8. *Always evaluate* yourself, the training materials, and the progress of the learners.

WHERE TO GO FOR MORE

One attribute of a trainer that has not been mentioned directly is that of constantly striving to become better at being a trainer. This is the characteristic of a true professional. It is the act of practicing what we preach: to continue to learn. The following are some resources for further learning.

Trainer training. These events are designed specifically for trainers, to help them to improve their skills. They are offered by University Associates, National Training Laboratories, and other academic and commercial organizations.

Professional organizations such as the American Society for Training and Development (ASTD), 600 Maryland Avenue S.W., Suite 305, Washington, DC 20024.

Formal Education. Many institutions offer courses of study and degree programs (bachelors, masters, doctorates) in instructional technology, organization development, and other aspects of human resource development. An excellent guide to many of them is found in the "Resources" section of *The 1982 Annual for Facilitators, Trainers, and Consultants* (J.W. Pfeiffer and L.D. Goodstein, Eds.), San Diego, CA: University Associates, 1982.

Publications of organizations and commercial training firms offer materials for trainer use and personal improvement.

Networks of various kinds, many of which are parts of or offshoots of professional and commercial organizations. An example is the OD Network, 1011 Park Avenue, Plainfield, New Jersey 07060.

- Reading Assignments - Possibly articles relating
  to the next lecture - answer ques. + turnin (15
- The. trng. module or 2-3 trng. module as a group. (50%)
- Final exam - lecture content (25%)
- Class participation - during lectures + trng. mod
  (10%)